DiDA
DIPLOMA IN DIGITAL APPLICATIONS

D203: Graphics
using Fireworks and Dreamweaver

R. Chasemore

PAYNE-GALLWAY

www.payne-gallway.co.uk

Acknowledgements

Published by Payne-Gallway Publishers
Payne-Gallway is an imprint of
Harcourt Education Ltd., Halley Court,
Jordan Hill, Oxford, OX2 8EJ

Copyright© Richard Chasemore 2006

First published 2006

11 10 09 08 07 06

10 9 8 7 6 5 4 3 2 1

British Library Cataloguing in Publication Data
is available from the British Library on request

10-digit ISBN: 1 904467 67 9

13-digit ISBN: 978 1 904467 67 0

Cover image© Richard Chasemore 2006

Design and Typesetting by Direction Marketing
and Communications Ltd

Printed by Printer Trento S.r.l

Ordering Information

You can order from:

Payne-Gallway,
FREEPOST (OF1771),
PO Box 381, Oxford OX2 8BR

Tel: 01865 888070
Fax: 01865 314029
E-mail: orders@payne-gallway.co.uk
Web: www.payne-gallway.co.uk

I must thank Pat Heathcote for editorial advice
and assistance in writing this book and Oliver
Heathcote for indexing it. I am indebted to
Flora and Robert Heathcote for permission
to use material from their books D202:
Multimedia and D204: ICT in Enterprise.

I am very grateful to Jamie Gardiner of Acorn
Adventure for kind permission to use the
following copyright images from the site
http://www.acornadventure.co.uk

CatamaranSailing	ArdecheRapid
Climbing	Abseiling
WigglyWorm	GorgeScrambling
RopeHighLeap	Squeezes
DeterminedKayaking	Archery
RaftBuilding	Rafting
CampSite	RockJumping

Many thanks to

- Hilary Craig for the use of the photograph
  TorOnDartmoor (used in the Dollar
  note image)
- Bill Byatt for his brilliant red eyes!
- Stuart Craig for his 1950s holiday picture.

Adobe product screenshots reprinted with
permission from Adobe Systems Incorporated.

Google screenshot p.58 copyright© Google.

Microsoft product screenshots reprinted with
permission from Microsoft Corporation.

Contents

Preface

About DiDA

DiDA (Diploma in Digital Applications) is a revolutionary series of qualifications launched by Edexcel in 2005, replacing GNVQ qualifications in ICT. As a suite of qualifications, it progresses from:

- Award (AiDA), consisting of Module D201, to
- Certificate (CiDA), consisting of Module D201 plus one other module, to
- Diploma (DiDA), consisting of Modules D201 to D204.

Each unit requires 90 guided learning hours.

The qualification places emphasis on real-life skills. All assessment is 'paperless': you will submit an electronic portfolio of work via Edexcel Online for onscreen moderation. A Summative Project Brief (SPB), supplied each year by Edexcel via their website, will guide you through a series of tasks to be performed.

About Unit D203

D203 is the Graphics unit. You will learn how to create original artwork for a wide variety of purposes, using Fireworks, one of the components of the Macromedia Studio suite. The screenshots have been taken using Studio 8, but instructions have been given for users of Studio MX where necessary – differences between versions are all minor.

You will display the artwork that you have created in an eportfolio, and detailed instructions are given on how to create this using Dreamweaver. As this is a graphics unit, great emphasis is put on creating a good-looking eportfolio which is itself a work of art. The sample eportfolio created to accompany this book can be downloaded from www.payne-gallway.co.uk/didaD203/eportfolio.

About this book

This book will teach you exactly what is required to do well in the Edexcel SPB. Planning, research and documentation skills are all covered, and Good Marks... Bad Marks... sections at the end of the appropriate chapters will help to ensure you know what is required to achieve top marks.

Mastering graphics software is a challenge to most students as well as to their teachers. With step-by-step instructions and hot tips from a professional graphic artist, you will soon be expert in using Fireworks and Dreamweaver!

Section One
LEARNING FIREWORKS

The Project

You will be given a scenario for this unit by Edexcel. You will need to do some research on the topic of the scenario, and produce various graphic components. You will then put all these components into an eportfolio, which will be assessed by the Exam Board; in Chapters 19 to 23 you will learn more about the eportfolio and how to put it together in Dreamweaver. You will be expected to spend a minimum of 30 hours on the project.

In order to practise the skills required for the set project, you will work through a sample project of a similar nature in this book. You can view the sample Summative Project Brief (SPB) at www.payne-gallway.co.uk/didaD203/spb and the finished eportfolio, similar to the one you will produce, at www.payne-gallway.co.uk/didaD203/eportfolio.

The Scenario

Base Camp is an activity club for children aged between 9 and 14. You have been asked to produce a range of graphic products for the club.

Figure 1.1   © Acorn Adventure

Graphics for the sample project

For the sample project, you must design and produce the following:

- **a logo for Base Camp**. For the logo, you must include a scan of your preliminary sketches, annotated to show how you developed your ideas. The logo must use at least three colours, be scalable without losing detail, and work in colour or monochrome.

- **a birthday card**, which will be given to children who have birthdays at the camp. It should be identifiable as a Base Camp birthday card. For this piece of work, you are also required to make a hand-drawn mock-up of the real card, photograph it and include this evidence of your design. You must show the dimensions and scale of the card, and show how you used a grid to ensure the picture was correctly positioned on the front of the card. You must show the finished version of the outside of the card.

- **a Base Camp dollar** note, which will be used instead of money inside the camp. You should explain how the image would be prepared for printing (specifying the resolution, size and colour system) so that it will look how you want it to. You are only required to design one side of the note.

- **a single web page advertising the camp**, which must contain a banner and three appropriate graphic images, including at least one which uses a secondary source that has been manipulated in some way.

You must ask suitable test users for feedback on each piece of artwork, and make changes when appropriate.

Planning your project

You must produce a detailed plan of how you will complete all the required tasks within the time allowed.

Before you start the plan:

- read through the project brief
- make a list of all the tasks to be completed
- break each task down into subtasks
- decide how long you think each subtask is going to take
- decide on the order in which the tasks need to be done
- identify which tasks you will do in class time, and which can be done at home
- decide at what points you need to get feedback and to evaluate your work so far.

At regular intervals, you must make sure that you are on schedule; if you are not, you must reschedule the remaining tasks into the time you have left to complete the project. **Keep a record of changes made to your schedule**.

Elements table

All the images that you use or create must be listed in a table, which you will include in your eportfolio. In the next chapter you will create an **Elements** table in Word. You will make entries in this table as you work through the project.

The project brief

The Summative Project Brief (SPB) is specified over several pages on Edexcel's website. When the time comes for you to start the SPB, you will have to explore the website and make a list, similar to the list below, of what you have to do.

You will put your artwork into an eportfolio to showcase your designs. You must include evidence of your design process, where this is specified, and add a commentary explaining how you achieved the final effect. This means you may have to save different versions of a piece as you work on it, and make notes so that you can annotate these versions.

You will also need to show your plan, and evidence of how you used the plan to complete your work.

Creating a project plan

Projects are unlikely to succeed unless they are properly planned. However, before you can start to plan, you have to be absolutely clear about the purpose of the project and what you are required to produce.

You should read the entire project brief first. There are a number of key questions you need to ask, including:

- what do I have to produce?
- what is it for?
- who is the intended audience?
- when do I have to have it finished?
- what resources can I use?
- how will the success of the project be judged?
- who will review my work and when?

You could use Word or Excel to produce a plan. This is a skill you will have learnt in D201. You should specify all the tasks and subtasks, and estimate how long each will take, when you will complete each one, and whether it will be done in class or at home. You can make changes to your plan as you go along; if you do, be sure that you will still meet the deadline, and make a note of why you had to adjust the plan. The plan and amendments have to be included in your eportfolio.

Project Plan

Project Start Date: _____   Project Due Date: _____

Task	Task Name	Subtask	Time allowed	Start Date	End Date	Home/ Class	Notes
1	Plan the project	Read the project brief					
		Create an organised folder structure for the project files					
		Produce a plan listing individual tasks, subtasks, estimated completion dates etc.					
	CHECKPOINT	*Check plan with teacher*					
2	Create logo	Collect stimulus material for corporate image, logo					
		Sketch some ideas					
		Scan the sketches to include in eportfolio					
		Create the logo					
		Get feedback					
		Make changes if necessary					
3	Birthday card	Gather stimulus material					
		Make mock-up and take photograph					
		Start card and take screenshot showing early version with grid					
		Complete front and back of card					
		Get feedback					
		Make changes if necessary					
	CHECKPOINT	*Check work with teacher*					
4	Web page	(fill in subtasks)					
5	Create eportfolio	(fill in subtasks)					

Figure 1.2: Project plan

Software

We will be using Macromedia Fireworks to create all the graphics for this project. The version that has been used in this book is Fireworks 8, but as it is very similar to Fireworks MX you will have no difficulty following the instructions whichever version you use.

The eportfolio will be created using Dreamweaver 8. These two packages are components of Studio 8, an updated version of Studio MX.

File-naming conventions

It is a good idea to decide on a convention for naming folders and files, and then to stick to it. For this project, all our folders and files will use 'CamelCaps': each word in the file or folder name will start with an uppercase letter, but we will not use spaces or underscores in file names.

Additional exercises

As you work through this book, you will learn many techniques and create many images, not all of which will be used in the final eportfolio. Therefore, you will need to create an extra folder (called **D203Exercises**) to hold all the other graphics you create.

Creating a folder structure

You need to create a folder structure to hold all the various graphics, documents, scans and source material that you accumulate during your project. This can be created using Windows Explorer. Here is the structure that we will use. The extra folder **D203Exercises** should be created outside this structure.

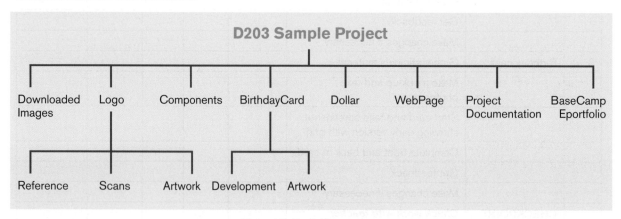

Figure 1.3: The folder structure

DownloadedImages

This folder will contain images that you download from various sources for use in your project. This might include, for example, photographs which you manipulate or use in a montage.

Logo

This folder will contain three subfolders: **Reference**, **Scans** and **Artwork**. **Reference** will be used to save other logos or graphics that you use as reference material to help you form your own ideas. **Scans** will be used to save scans of your hand-drawn sketches; at least one of these will be included in your eportfolio to show progression of ideas. **Artwork** will be used to save versions of the logo and any other artwork you develop as part of the corporate image.

Components

This folder will contain images that may be used in more than one piece of final artwork; for example, a montage that is used on a web page and on a birthday card.

BirthdayCard

This folder will contain two subfolders: **Development** and **Artwork**. You will be required to create and photograph a mock-up of your birthday card, and the photos can be saved into **Development**. You will also use this folder to save a screenshot of the grid you use. **Artwork** will be used to save the various versions of your birthday card.

Dollar

This folder will contain the artwork for your Base Camp Dollar.

WebPage

This folder will contain the components that you use in your web page advertising Base Camp, as well as the finished web page.

ProjectDocumentation

This folder will contain all the Word files, Excel files, screenshots and other files used to plan and monitor your project, such as your **ProjectPlan**, **ProjectReview** and **ProjectEvaluation**. These documents will be added to the eportfolio at the end of the project.

BaseCampEportfolio

This folder will contain HTML files created in Dreamweaver. You will add some subfolders to this folder later when you come to create the eportfolio.

Creating the folder structure

Create a folder structure in Windows Explorer. It should look like the one shown in Figure 1.4.

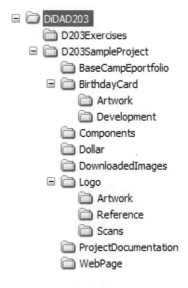

Figure 1.4

Elements table

You must keep a record of all the images you use or create in an **Elements** table. You can download this from the **Edexcel DiDA-D203** site (via the SPB), or create your own. It needs to be in Landscape format and have the columns shown in Figure 1.5.

Image (file name)	Primary/ Secondary Source	Bitmap/ Vector/ Combination	Description	Source Details	Produced by	Where used	Permission (how obtained if required)

Figure 1.5: Elements table

Good Marks... ✓

You will get good marks if you:

- read the SPB carefully and make a list of everything you need to do
- use a table, calendar or chart for your plan; it should include:
    - tasks and subtasks
    - a description of each task, and whether it will be done in class or at home
    - the date you will start each task
    - the date you will finish each task, and time allowed for each task
    - time for test users and reviewers to give feedback
    - checkpoints when you will talk to your teacher and assess your own progress
    - space for any notes relevant to each task
    - a sensible order for the tasks
    - extra time built in to your plan for emergencies or any problems
- agree your plan with your teacher
- meet your deadlines by sticking to your plan
- keep a record of the changes you make to the plan
- decide on a file-naming convention
- set up a logical folder structure
- keep details in the **Elements** table of all images used or created.

Bad Marks... ✗

You will lose marks if you:

- set yourself an unrealistic timetable
- produce your plan but don't use it
- produce your plan *after* you have completed your project
- produce a plan that is the same as everyone else's.

Getting Started

Fireworks is a versatile art package. You can use it to create, edit and optimise both bitmapped and vector images. It is primarily aimed at web designers, so you can quickly and easily create hyperlink buttons, rollover images and pop-up menus as well as creating and editing graphics using a range of effects.

Let's get started!

 Load Macromedia Fireworks 8. You can do this one of two ways:

- *Either* double-click the **Fireworks** icon on the Desktop

- *or* click **Start** at the bottom left of the screen, then click **Programs**. When the programs pop up, click **Macromedia** and then

 Macromedia Fireworks 8

Your screen will look like this:

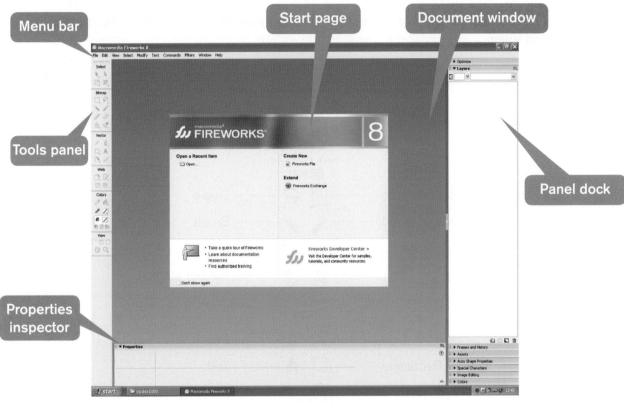

Figure 2.1: The opening screen

Menu bar: This contains menus organised by topic. The **Help** option on this menu is useful for getting extra information on a particular topic.

Tools panel: This is docked down the left side of the screen. This is where you will choose the tools to create or edit your pictures.

Properties inspector: This will initially show document information, and it will display options and properties when you select an **object** or **tool**.

Panel dock: This area contains a range of powerful **panels**. Panels can be opened and closed from the **Window** menu.

Document window: This is the workspace. It can be thought of as the artist's canvas.

Start page: This pops up when you start a new session with Fireworks, and displays recently opened items as well as shortcuts to download tutorials from the Macromedia site. You can click the **Don't show again** box to stop it from popping up.

The Tools panel

The **Tools** panel is organized into six sections or categories: **Select**, **Bitmap**, **Vector**, **Web**, **Colors** and **View**.

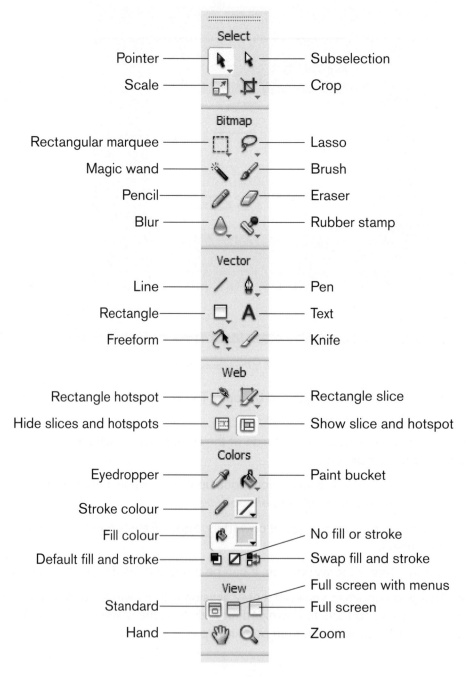

Pointer — Subselection

Scale — Crop

Rectangular marquee — Lasso

Magic wand — Brush

Pencil — Eraser

Blur — Rubber stamp

Line — Pen

Rectangle — Text

Freeform — Knife

Rectangle hotspot — Rectangle slice

Hide slices and hotspots — Show slice and hotspot

Eyedropper — Paint bucket

Stroke colour

Fill colour — No fill or stroke

Default fill and stroke — Swap fill and stroke

Full screen with menus

Standard — Full screen

Hand — Zoom

Figure 2.2: The Tools panel

Until a new document is opened, the **Tool** icons are grayed out. They will only become active when there is an open file.

Creating a new document

You can create a new file from the **Start Page** by selecting **Create New, Fireworks File**. Alternatively, go to the Menu bar and choose **File, New**.

 Create a new file now. The **New Document** window will appear showing default settings.

 Set the **Width** to **1000 Pixels**, the **Height** to **750 Pixels** and the **Resolution** to **72 Pixels/Inch**.

> ### Tip:
>
> 72dpi (dots per inch) is the norm for most computer screens, but if you are creating graphics for printing then you may need to use a higher resolution (common settings are 300dpi and 600dpi).

 Set the **Canvas color** to **White**. This is the most suitable colour for the image you are going to create.

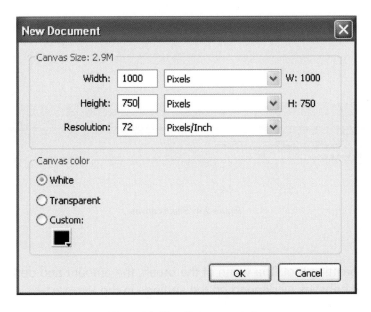

Figure 2.3: New Document window

> ### Tip:
>
> Make sure you have selected **Pixels** and **Pixels/Inch** in the drop-down lists. Fireworks may have initially assumed **Centimeters** and **Pixels/cm**.

 Click **OK**.

Your screen will look like this:

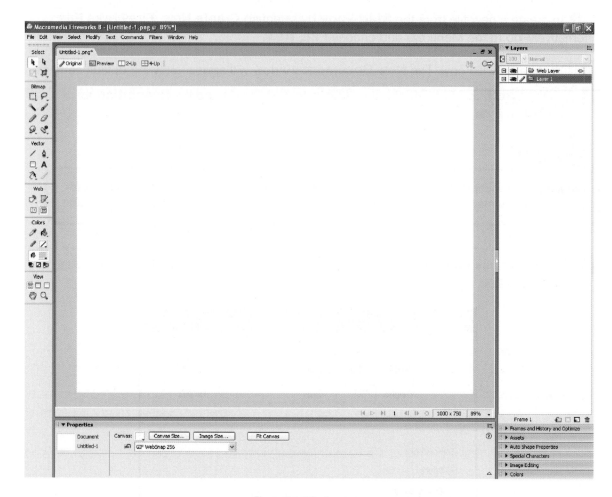

Figure 2.4: Blank canvas

The Brush tool

Brush Icon

The **Brush** tool is a painting tool. The width of the brush, the amount and density of the paint on the brush, and how it behaves all depend on the settings in the **Properties inspector**.

 Select the **Brush** tool from the **Tools** panel.

Click and drag the paintbrush on the canvas to see the effect.

 Tip:

If you press **Shift** whilst drawing with the **Brush** tool, the brush will be locked on a horizontal/vertical/45-degree plane. If you hold down the **Shift** key and click around the canvas, the **Brush** tool will draw a series of straight lines.

The **Properties inspector** is used to pick colours and options.

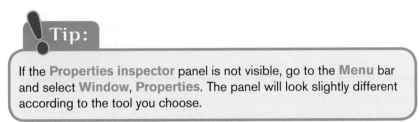

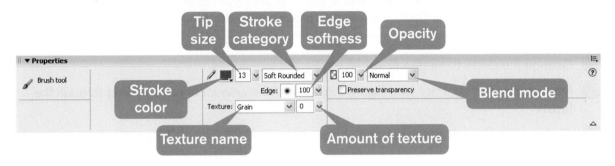

Figure 2.5: Properties inspector

On the bottom right of the **Properties inspector** there is a white triangle. Click it to switch between the full-size option and the half-size option.

Now collapse the **Properties inspector** by clicking the **black triangle** on the left of the **Properties inspector** title bar. Click it again to expand it. These options will be useful later when you have a more crowded workspace.

Click in the **Properties inspector** on the coloured square (the **Stroke color** box) and click on a colour from the pop-up window – something like a dark blue is best for the next stage.

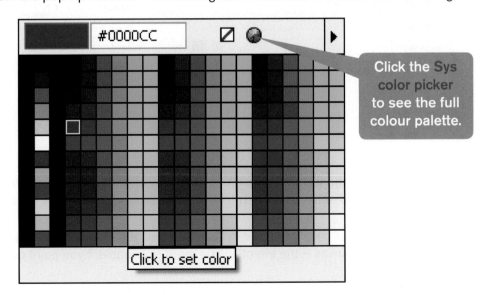

Figure 2.6: Colour pop-up window

15

Change the **Tip size** in the box next to the **Stroke color** box, and note that the brush changes size.

Tip:

When you click the **Tip size** box you will see a slider, which you can move up or down to increase or decrease the size of the brush. You can check the size of the brush by moving the mouse pointer over the canvas: an outline of the brush will show you its size and position. You can type a number in the **Tip size** box instead of using the slider if you find that quicker!

 Change the **Edge** to harden or soften the **Brush** tool edges.

 Now change the **Opacity** (see Figure 2.5) to alter the amount of paint flowing through the brush.

 Click the **Stroke category** box and choose **Charcoal, Textured.** Try painting!

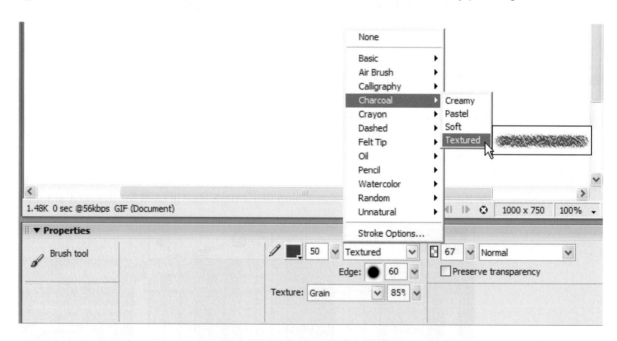

Figure 2.7: Choosing a Stroke category

 You can change the texture in the brush stroke by clicking the **Texture** box and choosing another texture. Use the slider next to it to increase or decrease the effect.

The **Blend mode** is something we will look at later, but you can try selecting different options and painting on the canvas – the effect will be more noticeable if you paint over lines you have already drawn.

The Zoom tool

Zoom Icon

▶ Click the **Zoom** tool (the bottom right icon in the **Tools** panel). You will notice the mouse pointer has turned into a magnifying glass with a plus sign in the middle.

▶ Click on your canvas to zoom in on your drawing so you can add some detail. Keep clicking as far as it will go.

Figure 2.8: Pixels

The squares that make up a picture are called pixels. When you created this canvas, you specified that it should be 1000 pixels wide and 750 pixels high.

▶ Press and hold the **Alt** key and notice that your magnifying glass now shows a minus sign. Click the canvas and you will zoom out.

▶ With the **Zoom** tool selected, right-click the canvas to access more options. If you choose **Magnification, 100%** you will go back to the original size. Another useful option is **Fit All**, to make the image exactly fill the window.

The Eyedropper tool

Eyedropper Icon

▶ Click the **Eyedropper** tool in the **Tools** panel. This tool will allow you to sample colours on your canvas. Click on a colour in the canvas to sample it, then click the **Brush** tool and paint – hey presto! You can change the stroke or fill colour, depending on which of these is selected in the **Colors** section.

▶ Select a fill colour and use the **Paint Bucket** tool to fill the area with this colour.

Paint Bucket Icon

Tip:

When you are using the **Brush** or **Paint Bucket**, you can press and hold the **Alt** key to quickly bring up the **Eyedropper** tool. When you release the **Alt** key, the original drawing tool is automatically reselected.

Undoing mistakes

If you don't like the last line you painted, you can undo it by going to the **Menu** bar and selecting **Edit**, **Undo Brush** tool, or you can press **Ctrl-Z**.

You can undo a whole lot of strokes using **Window**, **History** (**Shift-F10**). The **History** panel will appear in the **Panel** dock, and by using the slider on the left you can undo and redo several actions. Watch the results on the canvas as you slide.

Figure 2.9: History Panel

Save your first piece as **test1.png** in your **D203Exercises** folder, and close it.

Figure 2.10: Brush test

Using your new knowledge, make some new canvases (**1000** pixels by **750**) and draw some pictures. Save them in your **D203Exercises** folder – you may be able to use them in one of your projects!

Here are two that I created.

! Tip:

You can change the colour of the canvas when you open a new file by pressing **Custom** and choosing a new background colour.

Figure 2.11: Sample pictures

Maximising the workspace

A really good tip when working on a picture is to click the **Maximise** button in the top right of your canvas. This gives you a neutral border to paint across and when you zoom in, it shows you the maximum amount of picture on screen.

Minimise will put the canvas onto the bottom of the screen.

Maximise will fill the screen with the canvas and a border. Click this button again to restore it to its original size.

Close will close the canvas. It will ask if you would like to save your picture first.

Figure 2.12: The Minimise, Maximise and Close buttons. These will be grey if the workspace is already maximised.

Printing

From the **Menu** bar, select **File**, **Page Setup**.

Choose your printer's **Paper Size** and set the **Orientation** of the picture to **Landscape**. Press **OK** to confirm the changes.

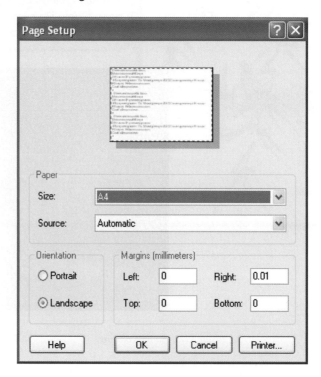

Figure 2.13: The Page Setup dialogue box

From the **File** menu select **Print**. The dialogue box is shown below.

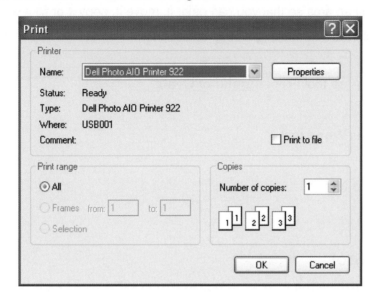

Figure 2.14: The Print dialogue box

You can now choose how many copies you want and press **OK** to print your favourite picture.

Select **File**, **Close** or click the **Close** button in the top right-hand corner of the canvas to close the picture.

Close Fireworks by clicking the **Close** button in the top right-hand corner of the window.

Making selections

A selection masks off an area so that you can paint it, move it, copy it or fill it with special effects.

There are three basic tools for making bitmap selections.

 The **Marquee** tool (**Rectangular** or **Oval**)

 The **Magic Wand** tool

 The **Lasso** tool

The Marquee tool

The **Marquee** tool enables you to make selections using either a rectangle or an oval (ellipse). We'll try them out.

 Create a new canvas with a **Width** of **500 Pixels**, a **Height** of **500 Pixels**, a **Resolution** of **72 Pixels/Inch**, and the **Canvas color** set to **White**.

Click the **Rectangular Marquee** tool.

Rectangular Marquee Icon

The **Properties inspector** for the **Marquee** tool may already be open. If it is not, click **Window** on the **Menu** bar and then click **Properties**.

Drawing with the Marquee tool

⊚ Set your options to match Figure 3.1.

Figure 3.1: Marquee tool options

⊚ Click on the canvas and draw out a rectangle (see Figure 3.3). The rectangle expands from the start point as you drag.

⊚ Draw a second rectangle, and you will see that the first one disappears. You can click and drag inside the rectangle to move the selection.

⊚ Select the **Paint Bucket** tool. Select a yellow colour, and check the settings are as shown in Figure 3.2.

Paint Bucket Icon

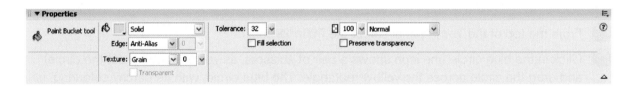

Figure 3.2: Paint Bucket tool options

⊚ Click in the selected rectangle – the area floods with yellow. Deselect the rectangle by clicking **Ctrl-D**.

⊚ Now click and hold the **Marquee** tool again and click the **Oval Marquee** tool option.

⊚ Set the **Edge** option in the **Properties inspector** to **Anti-Alias**. This will smooth the rounded selection.

⊚ Drag out a circle by holding down the **Shift** key after you have started drawing. (This technique can also be used to draw a square instead of a rectangle.)

 Tip:

You can also draw a rectangle or an ellipse with a fixed aspect ratio (width to height ratio) by changing the **Style** properties.

⊚ Use a large **Brush** tool, say **50** pixels, with opacity set to **30** to fill the circle roughly with blue. Keep clicking and releasing the mouse to add layers of paint (see Figure 3.3).

Brush Icon

Figure 3.3: Selecting and filling shapes

Important Note:

The black and white border around a selection is called a **marquee**. Sometimes it is referred to as the **marching ants**.

Moving a selection

Your blue circle should still be selected.

Pointer Icon

Subselection Icon

▶ From the top of the **Tools** panel select the **Pointer** tool.

▶ Click in the blue circle (the icon shows a pair of scissors, as you are cutting out the circle) and drag the circle across the yellow rectangle. The blue circle, with its patchy colouring, is moved.

▶ Click **Ctrl-Z** to undo the move, then click on the **Subselection** tool.

▶ Click in the blue circle and move it. Right away you will see that the icon has changed to a double arrow: this signifies you are dragging a copy of the blue circle.

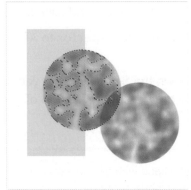

Figure 3.4: Dragging a copied selection

Tip:

Press **Shift** to constrain the angles or proportion of the move.

Transforming a selection

 With your copied circle still selected, choose **Modify**, **Transform**, **Free Transform** from the **Menu** bar. A box, called a **Transform box**, appears around the circle.

The little boxes around the edge of the **Transform box** are called **nodes**. See what happens when you place the mouse pointer over the nodes: the arrows show you in which direction you can stretch, resize or even spin the circle.

 Pull, stretch, resize and spin your selection. When you are finished experimenting, press **Enter.**

 Press **Ctrl-D** to deselect.

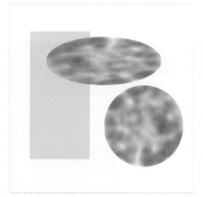

You can complete the transformation in a few different ways: press **Enter**, double-click inside the transformation box, or click on another tool.

Figure 3.5: Transforming a selection

You will notice that you can see through bits of the blue circle. This is because the canvas is not part of your picture: imagine your shapes are floating above the white background. This feature is useful, but you will need to remember that if you change the canvas colour it can be a very dramatic change.

 Go to the **Menu** bar and choose **Modify**, **Canvas**, **Canvas Color**.

 In the dialogue box that pops up, choose **Custom** and pick **black** from the pop-up window. Press **OK**. The canvas colour changes to black; big change!

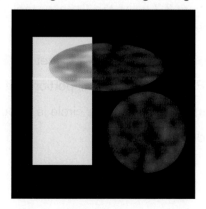

Figure 3.6: Changing the canvas colour

The Magic Wand tool

You can use the **Magic Wand** tool to select an area of a particular colour. You can set the **Tolerance** level so that colours which are almost but not quite the same will be selected.

The **Magic Wand** tool will only work with overlapping shapes if they are on the same layer (we will discuss layers in detail in Chapter 5). For now, we will just merge all of the layers into one.

Magic Wand Icon

- Press **Ctrl-A** to select all of the drawing objects, then, from the **Menu** bar, choose **Modify**, **Flatten Selection** (it's OK if this isn't available – that just means that everything is already on the same layer).

- Click the **Magic Wand** tool and then click in the yellow rectangle.

The portion of the rectangle not overlapped by the circle will be selected.

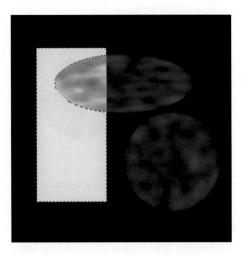

Figure 3.7: Selecting with the Magic Wand tool

Setting the Tolerance level

You could select the ellipse in Figure 3.7 using the **Pointer** tool, but we will experiment with setting the **Tolerance** level of the **Magic Wand**.

- In the **Properties inspector** for the **Magic Wand**, set the **Tolerance** to **10**.
- Click in the old blue circle. Probably only a small portion of it will be selected.
- Keep increasing the **Tolerance** until the whole circle is selected.
- Use the shortcut **Ctrl-D** to deselect.

Adding and subtracting selections

You add to selections by keeping the **Shift** key pressed while you make another selection.

▶ Experiment with this technique, selecting the circle and the part of the rectangle that isn't overlapped.

▶ You can close this image without saving – that's enough practice!

The Lasso tool

We will test some of our new skills by drawing a pattern of flowers using the **Selection** and **Brush** tools.

▶ Open a new canvas, and specify a **Custom** green background.

▶ Select the **Lasso** tool. By dragging the mouse pointer, draw a flower shape, as shown in Figure 3.8.

Lasso Icon

Don't forget you can have as many goes as you like to get it right. Just use the shortcut **Ctrl-D** to deselect, or click **Select** on the **Menu** bar and click on **Deselect**. This will deselect the flower so you can draw another flower shape.

Figure 3.8: Flower selection

Paint Bucket Icon

Oval Marquee Icon

Brush Icon

▶ Now select the **Paint Bucket** tool. Choose a white **Fill** colour. Move the mouse pointer over to the canvas, click and colour in the petals.

▶ Press **Ctrl-D**. You can now draw the next part of your picture.

▶ In the **Tools** panel, click on the **Marquee** tool and select the **Oval Marquee** tool.

▶ Draw a circle in the middle of the flower (remember to hold down **Shift**). You can use the arrow keys on the keyboard to nudge the selection into the perfect position, or you can drag the circle. Click the **Brush** tool and paint yellow in the circle selection (make sure the **Opacity** is set to **100**). Deselect when you have finished colouring.

Figure 3.9: Flower

Hopefully you will have a flower something like this! Now we are going to select the daisy and duplicate it all over the canvas.

Pasting daisies

Magic Wand Icon

▶ Click the **Magic Wand** tool and select the yellow centre.

▶ Keep **Shift** held down while you click in the white part of the flower to select it. You may have to click in several petals if your yellow circle overlaps them.

▶ Press **Ctrl** and **Alt** together, then click inside your selection and drag a duplicate of the flower onto the green canvas. Release the mouse, then click and drag again several times to arrange the flowers on the canvas.

Remember you can click **Ctrl-Z** to undo as many actions as you want!

Figure 3.10: Lots of daisies

Save your picture as **Daisies.png**.

You can use the **Magic Wand** tool to change the background colour. Then you can paint some shadows under the daisies using a soft brush, a slightly darker shade and a low opacity.

Try creating some other masterpieces!

Figure 3.11: Variations on a theme

Cloning

The **Rubber Stamp** tool is very powerful and is one of the most frequently used implements in the world of professional photo retouchers and computer artists. You'll need to spend some time playing around with it to understand how it works.

 Create a new canvas with a Width of **500 Pixels**, a **Height** of **500 Pixels**, a **Resolution** of **72 Pixels/Inch**, and choose a **Custom** purple canvas colour.

We are going to make a cartoon mad pig's face, something like the one in Figure 4.1.

Figure 4.1

We will start with the pig's eyes.

*Oval Marquee
Icon*

 In the **Tools** panel, click the **Oval Marquee** tool and draw an oval roughly where I have drawn the pig's left eye.

 Choose a soft-edged **Brush** tool and set the brush size to **100**, opacity **100%**. (**Opacity** determines how 'thickly' the paint is laid on. The higher the opacity, the thicker the paint.)

Brush Icon

 Paint the eye white.

Now we need a purple slightly darker than the background.

*Eye Dropper
Icon*

 Choose the **Eye Dropper** tool and click the purple background.

 Now select the **Brush** tool and you will notice the **Properties inspector** shows the purple colour. Click on the **Color** box. (See Figure 4.2.)

Click the **Sys color picker** to bring up the **Color pop-up** window. On the right-hand side, slide the bar down to darken your colour, and then click **OK**.

Sys color picker Icon

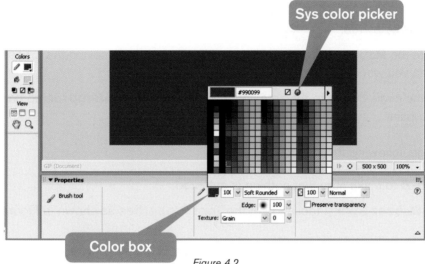

Figure 4.2

Reduce the size of the **Brush** tool to **60** and carefully spray a shadow area at the bottom of the eye. I would set the **Opacity** to **10** before you start to spray the shadow, so you can build up the colour without overdoing it.

Deselect (**Ctrl-D**) and draw a circle selection to make the pupil. Colour it black, and think about where you are placing it because you could make a big difference in the character's expression!

Spray a white highlight over the pupil to give it a sparkle: make the brush size **30** and the opacity **100%**, and just give it one burst of highlight.

Figure 4.3: Eye eye!

Tip:

Remember that you can press **Ctrl-Z** or select **Edit**, **Undo** from the menu to undo an action and try again!

*Rubber Stamp
Icon*

Using the Rubber Stamp tool

You can use the **Rubber Stamp** tool to paint an exact copy of any part of an image.

Once you have selected the **Rubber Stamp** tool, there are three stages to using it:

- Set the **Properties**.
- Activate the **Rubber Stamp** tool by pressing the **Alt** key, moving the crosshair over the area you want to clone (in this case the eye) and clicking.
- Move the circle cursor to the area you want your **Rubber Stamp** tool to paint, and click to paint.

Now give it a go, following the instructions below.

◉ Press **Ctrl-D** to make sure that nothing is selected.

◉ Click the **Rubber Stamp** tool and set the **Tool Properties** as shown in Figure 4.4.

Figure 4.4: Rubber Stamp properties

◉ Press and hold the **Alt** key and click somewhere in the pig's eye to activate the **Rubber Stamp** tool. Release the **Alt** key again.

◉ Move the mouse pointer to the position you want to **Rubber Stamp** a new eye! If the eye is in the wrong position, this will give you a chance to practise moving a selection.

◉ Start painting in small circles to clone the eye.

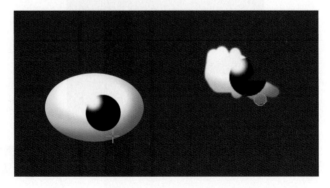

Figure 4.5: Starting to Rubber Stamp the eye

◉ Finish cloning the eye.

Moving a selection

The eye in Figure 4.5 is too high, and needs to be moved.

When the whole eye is selected, the **Marquee** tool changes shape to that of the **Marquee Move** tool as it passes over the selection.

Try it as follows:

 Use the **Magic Wand** to select the white part of the right eye. Then hold down **Shift** while you select the pupil.

Magic Wand Icon

Don't forget you can change the magic wand tolerance so you can more easily select the gradients.

 Now click the **Pointer** tool (or press **Ctrl** and the arrow keys) and move the eye. You should see something like Figure 4.6.

Pointer Icon

Figure 4.6: Moving a selection

It is quite usual to find that the **Magic Wand** misses some of the selection, so that a trace of the object is left in the original position. We can fix that now.

 From the **Select** menu, choose **Select Inverse**.

 Using the **Eraser** tool, carefully erase the leftover bits.

 Deselect by pressing **Ctrl-D**.

Eraser Icon

Subtracting selections

You already know how to add selections by holding down **Shift** as you make a second or third selection. You can also subtract portions of a selection by holding down the **Alt** key.

We will paint the mouth using this technique.

Oval Marquee Icon

▶ Click the **Oval Marquee** tool and draw a large oval selection (see Figure 4.7).

▶ Now hold the **Alt** key down and draw another oval starting from near the left eye.

The second oval has eaten away at the first oval, giving us a neat mouth shape.

▶ You can drag the selection, or use the arrow keys, to move the selection if you need to.

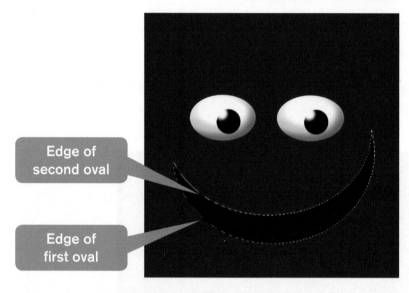

Figure 4.7: Subtracting selections

Important Note:

You will probably need several goes to get a shape you like. It is worth the effort.

▶ Use the **Brush** tool to spray the mouth dark purple and, decreasing the **Opacity** to about **20**, spray a small amount of the canvas colour on the bottom lip.

Tip:

When you airbrush fine gradients, build them up in fine layers and you will get a much better result.

34

Modifying a selection

Sometimes the selection area is almost, but not quite, what you want. You can modify it.

▶ From the **Select** menu, choose **Contract Marquee**. Set the **Contract Marquee** window to **10** pixels and press **OK**. You should see that the selection has got smaller.

▶ Go back to **Select** and this time go to **Feather**. Set the **Feather Radius** to **4** pixels and press **OK**. This will give a soft edge to the selection.

▶ Colour the selection so that it looks something like Figure 4.8.

Figure 4.8: A contracted, feathered selection. Note the soft edge to the mouth.

▶ Now select the **Lasso** tool and, holding down the **Alt** key, cut out some tombstone teeth like the ones in Figure 4.9.

Lasso Icon

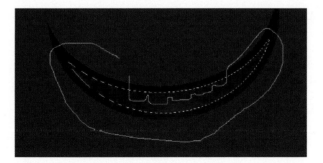

Figure 4.9: Cutting out the teeth

▶ With the **Brush**, paint the teeth a grimy colour. You can use the **Sys color picker** and the pop-up **Color** window to get a really bad tooth colour.

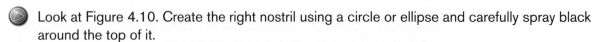

*Oval Marquee
Icon*

*Rubber Stamp
Icon*

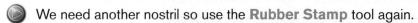

Use the **Oval Marquee** tool to draw the pig's nose, and then drag the selection to place it slightly over the right eye. Colour it a lighter purple than the background.

Look at Figure 4.10. Create the right nostril using a circle or ellipse and carefully spray black around the top of it.

We need another nostril so use the **Rubber Stamp** tool again.

Figure 4.10: Adding the nostrils

If you look at Figure 4.11, you will see I have made the pig slightly 3-D on the face by spraying lighter purple above the nose and dark purple under it.

Magic Wand Icon

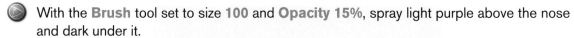

Click the **Magic Wand** tool and, with the **Tolerance** set very low, select the purple background.

With the **Brush** tool set to size **100** and **Opacity 15%**, spray light purple above the nose and dark under it.

Brush Icon

Finishing touches

You can use the **Lasso** tool to add the ears, some manic eyebrows in black and lastly some hair.

Figure 4.11: Pig

What a masterpiece! Well, maybe not…

 Save it as **MadPig.png** in your **D203Exercises** folder.

Layers are like transparent sheets arranged on top of each other. They can be arranged in different orders, and switched on and off. You can even make the layers react to different colours or contrasts and blend together to make some spectacular pictures.

Layers enable you to work on one element of your picture without changing the other elements and without having to make selections.

Figure 5.1: Layers

Create a new canvas with a **Width** of **600 Pixels**, a **Height** of **700 Pixels**, a **Resolution** of **72 Pixels/Inch**, and the **Canvas color** set to **White**.

Look at the **Layers** panel on the right. It should look like Figure 5.2.

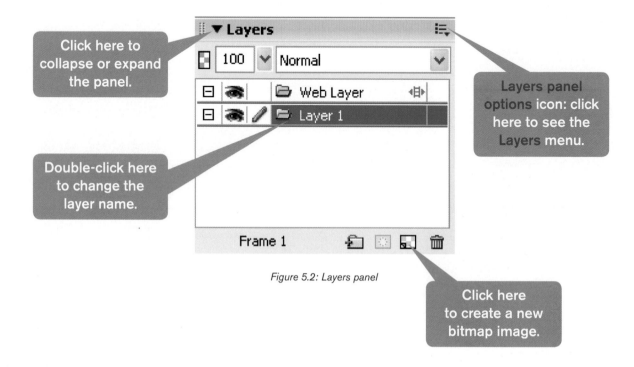

Figure 5.2: Layers panel

The top layer in the **Layers** panel is always the **Web** layer. This contains Web objects such as **hotspots**, **slices** and **rollovers**. When you create any of these objects in any layer, they are automatically placed in the **Web** layer. You will try this out in Chapter 17.

The current layer name (**Layer 1**) is coloured blue in the **Layers** panel.

You need to be able to see the whole canvas.

▶ Select **View**, **Fit All** from the **Menu** bar.

Before you can paint the canvas, you have to insert a new bitmap image on the current layer.

New Bitmap Icon

▶ Click the **New Bitmap Image** icon at the bottom of the **Layers** panel (see Figure 5.2.). Notice the new bitmap object appear under **Layer 1**.

▶ Click and hold the **Paint Bucket** tool. Select the **Gradient** tool, and match the **Gradient** tool **Properties inspector** to Figure 5.3. (The **Texture** box can be set to anything as no texture will be applied if the box next to it is set to zero.)

Paint Bucket Icon

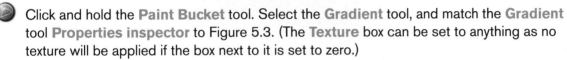

Figure 5.3: Paint bucket options

▶ Click the **Fill color** box and select **Preset: Blue, Red, Yellow**.

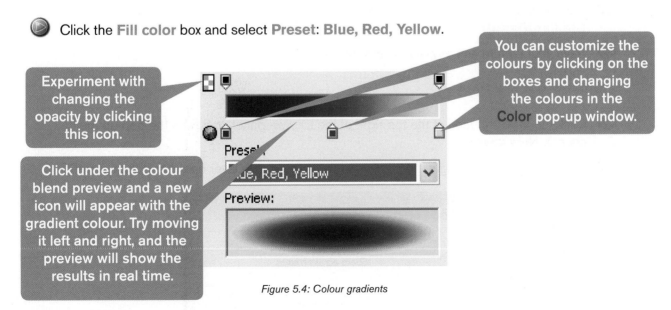

You can customize the colours by clicking on the boxes and changing the colours in the Color pop-up window.

Experiment with changing the opacity by clicking this icon.

Click under the colour blend preview and a new icon will appear with the gradient colour. Try moving it left and right, and the preview will show the results in real time.

Figure 5.4: Colour gradients

Click in the canvas; you should see a gradient pattern like Figure 5.5.

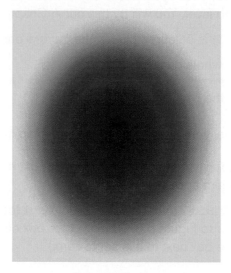

Figure 5.5: Gradient

Naming layers

It is a good idea to rename your layers as you go, so that you know at a glance what is on each layer.

Double-click on the name **Layer 1** in the **Layers** panel. Rename the layer **GradientBackground**.

Save your picture as **Layers.png** in your **D203Exercises** folder.

Making a new layer

Options Icon

Click the **Options** icon at the top right of the **Layers** panel, and from the pop-up menu choose **New Layer**.

In the **New Layer** dialogue box, enter **Rectangles** as the layer name, and then click **OK**.

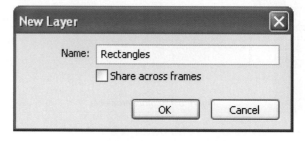

Figure 5.6: The New Layer dialogue box

This is what you should see in the **Layers** panel.

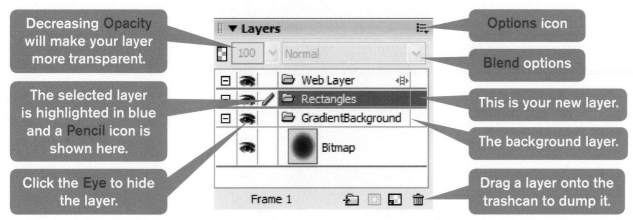

Decreasing Opacity will make your layer more transparent.

The selected layer is highlighted in blue and a Pencil icon is shown here.

Click the Eye to hide the layer.

Options icon

Blend options

This is your new layer.

The background layer.

Drag a layer onto the trashcan to dump it.

Figure 5.7: The Layers panel

◉ Select the **Rectangles** layer by clicking on it (it will be coloured blue when selected).

◉ With the **Rectangles** layer selected, pick the **Rectangular Marquee** tool and draw a rectangle. Keep the **Shift** key pressed down while you draw a complex criss-cross pattern of boxes. In the **Layers** panel, you will see the new **Bitmap** object appear in the **Rectangles** layer.

◉ Select the **Paint Bucket** tool, and change the **Fill Category** in the **Properties inspector** from **Ellipse** to **Solid**.

◉ Pour a colour that really clashes with the background. The **Layers** panel will show what is on the **Rectangles** layer.

Rectangular Marquee Icon

Paint Bucket Icon

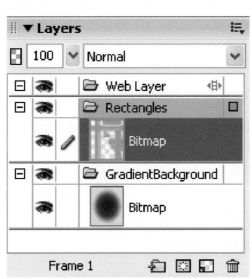

Figure 5.8

◉ Press **Ctrl-D** to deselect.

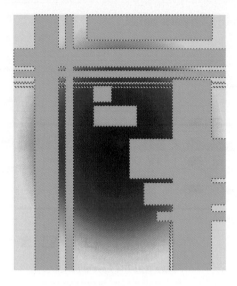

Figure 5.9: Filled pattern

New/Duplicate Icon

New Bitmap Icon

▶ Make a new layer. You can do it a different way this time, by pressing the **New/Duplicate layer** icon at the bottom of the **Layers** panel.

▶ If you have renamed the other two layers, the new layer will be called **Layer 1**. Double-click its name in the **Layers** panel and change its name to **BlackCircle**.

▶ Make sure **BlackCircle** is selected in the **Layer** panel.

▶ Click the **New Bitmap Image** button at the bottom of the **Layers** panel. If you forget to do this, you will automatically start drawing on one of the other layers.

▶ Select the **Oval Marquee** tool and hold down the **Shift** key while you draw a large circle right in the middle of the canvas. Colour it black with the **Paint Bucket** tool.

▶ Press **Ctrl-D** to deselect.

Understanding layers

We'll experiment with these three layers to gain an understanding of how they work.

▶ The different layers in your canvas appear in the same order as the names in the **Layers** panel.

▶ Drag the layers so that they appear in the order **Rectangles**, **BlackCircle**, **GradientBackground**.

The black circle is now under the criss-cross pattern. If you were to put it under **Gradient** background it would be completely covered.

Eye Icon

▶ Click the **Eye** icon and switch off and on all the layers.

With all the layers switched off, all you can see is the white canvas colour. As you have made your own background to cover the canvas, it would not make any difference to the final image if you had a transparent background. You can try this:

 From the **Menu** bar, select **Modify, Canvas, Canvas Colour** and choose **Transparent.** You will notice that Fireworks shows a checkerboard pattern to show nothing is there.

Manipulating images on different layers

 With the **BlackCircle** layer selected, pick the **Pointer** tool and move the circle anywhere you like. Try moving **Rectangles** as well – you will see that each layer can be moved or shuffled in any order you like.

 Now use the **Opacity** slider in the **Layers** panel and experiment with the layers. Set them back to **100** when you are finished.

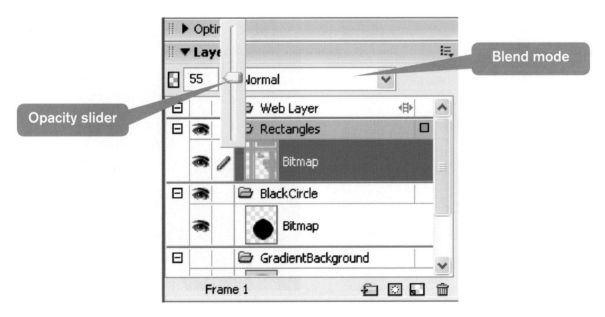

Figure 5.10: Layer opacity

 Experiment with the **Blend mode**, currently set to **Normal.**

I set the **Blend mode** for **Rectangles** to **Difference** and that for **BlackCircle** to **Hue.**

43

Figure 5.11: Blend modes

Figure 5.12: Some different effects

Try making some other funky backgrounds!

Save your pictures as **Layers2.png**, **Layers3.png**, and so on, in the **D203Exercises** folder.

Chapter 6 – Vector Graphics

Raster or bitmap images are made up from a grid of coloured pixels. The resolution of a picture is typically measured in pixels per inch (ppi – on screen) or dots per inch (dpi – on paper), and the more pixels per inch, the finer the detail in the picture. Raster images are very good for storing and changing photographic pictures, but, if you enlarge the image, the results will probably not be satisfactory and individual pixels will be visible.

Vector images are made from mathematical information about the curves, sizes, and point positions and colours. Whenever you change the size of a vector image, rotate it or skew the image, it is redrawn and will be perfect. This type of image is good for graphical shapes or text. We are now going to create a vector image which can be used at any size in a variety of printed materials, such as a brochure, birthday card, postcard or poster as well as on a website.

We will need a mascot to add a bit of fun to the Activity Club marketing materials, so meet Base Camp Bunny!

Starting the vector rabbit

- Create a new canvas with a **Width** of **600 Pixels**, a **Height** of **800 Pixels**, a **Resolution** of **72 Pixels/Inch**, and the **Canvas color** set to a **Custom** very light grey.

- Locate the **Vector** tool section in the **Tools** panel. Select the **Ellipse** tool. (It is on the same button as the vector **Rectangle** tool.)

Ellipse Icon

- Have look in the **Properties inspector** shown in Figure 6.1. You will notice it has **Fill** (**Paint Bucket** tool) and **Stroke** (**Pencil** tool) colour boxes.

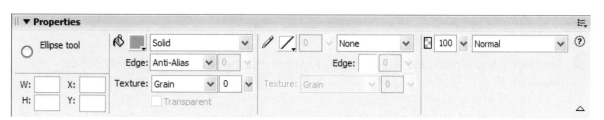

Figure 6.1: Vector properties

- Click in the **Fill color** box and choose medium grey, **#999999**: this will now be the colour inside the vector shape.

Fill color Icon

Stroke color Icon

- Leave the **Stroke** colour as **Transparent**. This means there will be no pencil line around the shape we are about to draw.

- Click and drag an ellipse on the canvas.

Pointer Icon

○ You can adjust, move and rotate the vector ellipse in several different ways. If you click on the **Pointer** tool, you can move the ellipse. Now click on the **Subselection** tool next to it, and you will be able to click and move any of the four nodes.

○ Undo your changes by using **Ctrl-Z**, or delete the ellipse and draw another one. This time, from the **Menu** bar select **Modify**, **Transform**, **Free Transform**. You can now move, resize and rotate the ellipse in any way.

○ Try to match Figure 6.2, and then press **Enter** or double-click to finish.

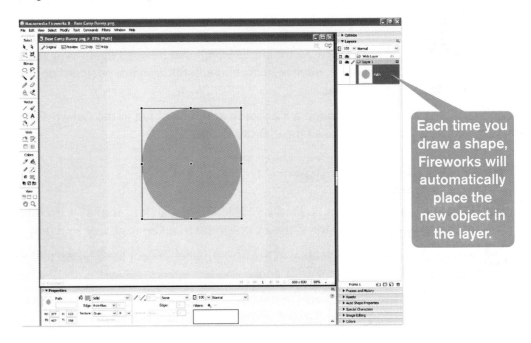

Each time you draw a shape, Fireworks will automatically place the new object in the layer.

Figure 6.2: Story so far!

○ The ellipse has a pale blue line around it to show that it is selected. Press **Ctrl-D** to deselect.

When you pass the mouse pointer over the ellipse, a red line appears around the ellipse to show that it is a vector shape, but is not currently selected. Try reselecting it with the **Pointer** tool and then deselecting again.

The ellipse you have just drawn will be the rabbit's head. We are going to add his eyes next.

○ Draw a nice big white eye, as shown in Figure 6.3.

○ Position it with the **Pointer** tool, if necessary.

○ Hold down **Ctrl** and **Alt** while you drag to duplicate the eye. If you also press the **Shift** key this will lock the duplicated shape in a horizontal or vertical plane.

○ Draw another ellipse with a black fill to make the pupil in the eye, and duplicate it to the other eye.

46

Now for the cheeks. Draw a white ellipse, duplicate it and move it over a bit, so that it overlaps the first ellipse. Note that you are creating a new object called **Path** in **Layer 1** with each shape.

Figure 6.3: Building the bunny in stages

We can make these two ellipses into a single shape. Click the **Pointer** tool and keep the **Shift** pressed while you select the first ellipse, so that both ellipses are selected.

From the **Menu** bar, select **Modify**, **Combine Paths**, **Union**. The two cheeks combine to form a single vector shape or **Path**.

Now that the cheeks are one vector shape, see if you can copy this shape, make it smaller, colour it pink and move it into position to make part of the nose, as shown in Figure 6.4. Draw a red circle to finish the nose.

Figure 6.4: Combined paths

Draw another ellipse and colour it purple. It needs to be underneath the cheeks, so look in the **Layers** panel and drag the object (**Path**) down under the pink-coloured nose. Look at Figure 6.5 for inspiration!

Rounded Rectangle Icon

 Use the **Rounded Rectangle** tool (on the same button as the vector **Ellipse** tool) to make some light yellow teeth, and rotate them slightly to make them look more 'buck'. Move the teeth layers between the pink nose layer and the purple mouth layer.

Figure 6.5: Buck teeth

Naming layers

Your **Layers** panel probably looks something like Figure 6.6 at this stage. By default, Fireworks gives names like **Path**, **Rounded Rectangle** to each vector object. (Bitmap objects are named **Bitmap** by default.)

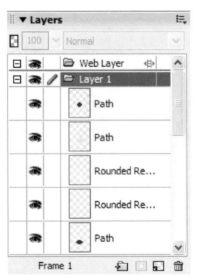

Figure 6.6

It is a good idea to rename the objects to indicate what is on each layer. Double-click the layer name to do this.

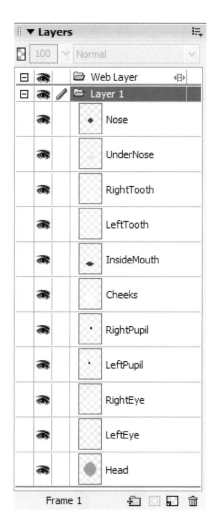

Figure 6.7: Layers panel

⊙ Before we complete the last bit, you can resize and reposition the drawing. First, select the whole image by dragging around it with the **Pointer** tool.

⊙ Then select **Modify**, **Transform**, **Free Transform** (or use the shortcut **Ctrl-T**) to make the rabbit's head about half the canvas height and position it near the bottom of the canvas.

Copying and pasting objects

Now you nccd to draw the ears.

⊙ Draw and position the first ear shape as a rotated ellipse (see Figure 6.8).

⊙ To get the same colour you used for the face, click the **Fill color** box and move the mouse pointer over the rabbit so that the mouse pointer changes into an **Eyedropper** tool. Click on the mid-grey of the rabbit's head.

⊙ Select the **Pointer** tool, click the ear shape and from the **Menu** bar select **Edit**, **Copy** (or press **Ctrl-C**).

Eyedropper Icon

▶ Now select **Edit**, **Paste** (or press **Ctrl-V**).

▶ The pasted copy will appear on top of the first ellipse. Click and drag it to its new position, and rotate it using **Modify**, **Transform**, **Free Transform**.

Tip:

If your ears cover the eyes, drag the layers all the way to the bottom. Or you could use **Modify**, **Arrange**, **Send to Back**.

Figure 6.8: Ear we go!

▶ Make two pink ellipses to put inside the ears (see Figure 6.9).

▶ Use the **Subselection** tool to customise the insides of the ears. Click the ellipse with the Subselection tool, click the bottom node (it will turn blue) and drag it up to flatten the bottom of the ellipse.

▶ Make a droopy ear with another ellipse the same colour as the ears, making sure it goes over the top of the pink ear pieces.

▶ Use the vector **Line** tool to add some whiskers.

Figure 6.9: Base Camp Bunny

You will probably find that some of your objects are not quite correctly positioned. Use the **Pointer** tool to select an object that you want to move, or right-click and choose **Transform**, **Scale** to make bigger changes.

Remember too that you can select several shapes at once by holding down **Shift** while you select each one.

 Save your vector artwork as **BaseCampBunny.png** in the **Components** folder.

Layer Styles

Right, let's add some fantastic **filters**; these can transform your vector illustration in moments.

 Start by selecting the round nose by clicking on it with the **Pointer** tool.

 Find **Filters** (**Effects** in Fireworks MX) at the bottom right of the **Properties inspector**.

 Click the + sign; choose **Shadow and Glow**, **Drop Shadow**, and choose settings as shown in Figure 6.10. The changes will be applied as you change the settings.

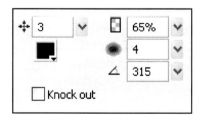

Figure 6.10: Drop shadow options

Click on the canvas to apply the drop shadow.

 Click the + sign to add another filter: **Eye Candy 4000 LE, Bevel Boss.**

 Match the settings to Figure 6.11. Click the **Lighting** and **Bevel Profile** tabs and have a play to get a really rounded shiny nose! Press **OK** to apply the changes.

> **Tip:**
>
> The lighting angle controls the light source direction. The bevel profile will help give your object a real three-dimensional quality, so always adjust it to achieve the best possible effect.

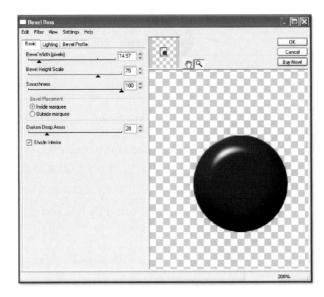

Figure 6.11: Eye Candy nose!

Isn't that great?

 Click the other shapes and add drop shadows or a little bit of moulding to make the rabbit a bit more three-dimensional.

If you change your mind about a filter, you can turn it off temporarily or delete it altogether – see Figure 6.12.

Click the tick and your filter will be temporarily switched off – try it! Select a filter and click the – sign to delete the effect altogether.

Click on the i and the Options box will pop up so you can edit the filters.

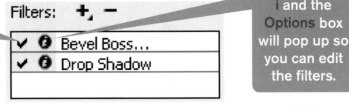

Figure 6.12: Editing your filters

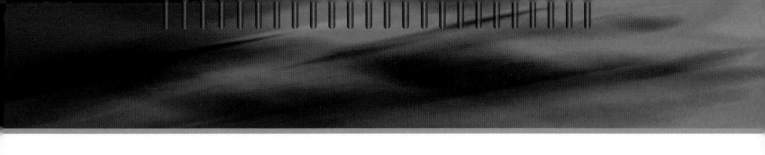

 Save your picture with a different name: **BaseCampBunny3d.png**.

Figure 6.13: Finished bunny

Vector vs. raster images

When you draw a shape, or write some text using the **Text** tool, the shapes and text are **vector** graphics. When you use the **Brush** tool to spray a bit of the canvas, this is a **bitmap** or **raster** image.

Enlarging or resizing

Vector images are independent of resolution; the computer remembers the geometrical information associated with that shape, and if the resolution or image size is changed, the shape can simply be redrawn with no loss of image quality. The extra information that allows the software to do this is called embedded information.

Raster images, because they are stored as a collection of different-coloured pixels, will become pixilated if they are enlarged too much. This is why you should always enlarge a vector image to its final size before you turn it into a raster image, not after.

The **BaseCampBunny** is a **vector** image. The **MadPig** you created in Chapter 4 is a **raster** image. We'll look at what happens when we zoom in and resize each image.

 Open your **BaseCampBunny.png** (which should have no effects applied to it) and your **MadPig.png** files. The two file names will appear on the tabs at the top of the canvas, and you can click a tab to see the image.

 Zoom in on both pictures in turn, as far as the zoom will go.

Zoom Icon

You will see both images have pixilated edges. This is because computer monitors display images on a grid made up of pixels, which means that although vector images should appear with perfect smooth edges, the data is displayed as pixels on screen

Now see what happens when we make the canvas bigger.

 Start with MadPig. Reset the picture to 100% zoom – the magnification factor is shown in the blue Title bar (you can do this quickly by pressing Ctrl-1).

 Select Modify, Canvas, Image Size from the Menu bar.

 Copy the width and height settings from Figure 6.14. Click OK.

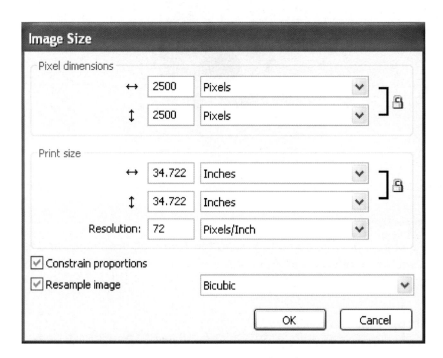

Figure 6.14: Image size settings for the raster image

The image has increased in size. Notice that the image is quite blurred. This is because, to show the raster image at this size, Fireworks divided up the existing pixels, since there is no more information stored in the image.

Figure 6.15: The raster image is blurred

Now click on the BaseCampBunny image. Reset the picture to 100% zoom.

Select Modify, Canvas, Image Size from the Menu bar.

Copy the settings from Figure 6.16.

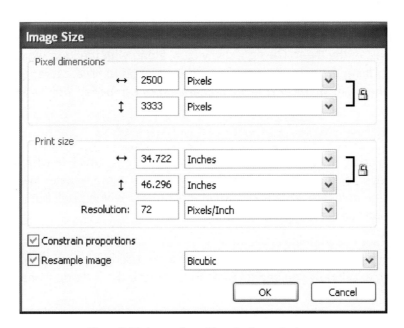

Figure 6.16: Image size settings for the vector image

Zoom in and have a look.

Figure 6.17: The vector image is sharp after resizing

The edges are still sharp because the shape information embedded in the vector image has been used to re-draw the image at a larger size.

 Close both images without saving.

 In Word, make an entry in your **Elements** table for **BaseCampBunny**, which is from a primary source (since you created it).

We will be using the bunny in the birthday card and other artwork. It will be one of the recognizable symbols of the **Base Camp** activity club, along with the logo which we will develop in the next chapter. Using the same image over and over helps to create a recognizable brand. Can you think of other companies which use a character or symbol as well as a logo?

Converting vector images into raster images

There are certain things that you cannot do with vector graphics, which is why we sometimes need to simplify a layer, or **flatten** an image. Doing this turns it into a raster layer or raster image. When you do this, the software remembers which colour is in which pixel, but it no longer knows where one shape ends and another one starts.

If you imagine a vector image being a pile of shapes that can be individually picked up and moved around, turning that vector image into a raster image is like taking a photo of all the shapes; the image looks the same, but now you cannot pick up and move the individual shapes.

Chapter 7 – Creating a Logo

You will need to do some background work before you start designing components for your project. All graphic designers and illustrators have huge libraries of source material; anything you see and like you should collect and store, so that you can browse through your collection when you are searching for inspiration. Your library of source material might take the form of a list of favourites in your Web browser, or a folder containing graphics you have downloaded and information about where you found them. For the SPB, you must make a note in the **Elements** table of all the images you use or create (see Chapter 1, Figure 1.5, page 8).

Before you start designing the Base Camp logo, you need to think about such things as:

- What it is for?

- Who it is for?

- How it is going to be used?

- What typeface would be appropriate?

For this project, you have to design a logo for an outdoor adventure centre called Base Camp. It should be designed to appeal to children aged about 9 to 14.

The logo will be used in different advertising materials, so it needs to be identifiable as outdoors-based, and it needs to be bright and fun so that kids can relate to it. Also, a good logo can be used for T-shirts, stickers and mugs, and can become a cool symbol of its brand. (You are probably wearing at least one item with a logo!)

Look at the website **http://graphicdesign.about.com/od/designinglogos/tp/logotips.htm** for top tips on designing logos. Here are the main points:

- Keep it simple.

- Do your research: look at other company logos and decide what you like and don't like about them.

- Design in black and white initially.

- Make sure your company name is clear.

- Choose colours carefully.

- Choose typeface carefully.

- Make sure it works in a variety of sizes.

- Pause to reflect, and come back to it in a week to see if you still like it. Check it for typos!

- Avoid clip art.

- Do a mock-up of your logo where it will be used (in documents, on signs, on a vehicle, and so on) to see if it works.

Collecting secondary components

A word about copyright

There is a huge amount of material available on the web, and you should take advantage of it. A lot of websites are happy for you to download free resources provided they aren't for commercial use (that is, you aren't going to profit financially from using them). If you are using resources for a school or college assignment then there is no need to seek permission for each component used. If you decide to publish a book using these components then clearly you must ask permission.

Copying images from other websites

The best way to search for images on a particular subject is to use a search engine. Google is particularly useful because it can search specifically for images.

Load Internet Explorer then go to the Google homepage (www.google.co.uk or www.google.com). Type the search criteria Logo then click Google Search.

You'll find there are plenty of sites that give advice on developing logos.

Figure 7.1 Google splash page

Now have a look at some sample logos: click where it says Images at the top of the screen.

If you find a suitable image, click on it to visit the website it originates from. Right-click it then select Save Picture As from the menu that appears.

Save the picture in your Logo\Reference folder.

58

Designing the logo

I have been on the Internet and found some logos that I like and think will appeal to kids. I've looked at magazines for lovers of extreme sports such as snowboarding, mountain biking, mountaineering, kite surfing and canoeing.

The next stage is to start sketching logos. Most importantly, add your text. There are endless possible variations, but the rule of thumb is 'if it looks right, it is right, and if it looks wrong, chuck it away and start again.' I have, on occasion, spent days trying to make something work, only for the client to tell me what I already knew: 'It doesn't look right!'

With pen and paper, start to sketch ideas.

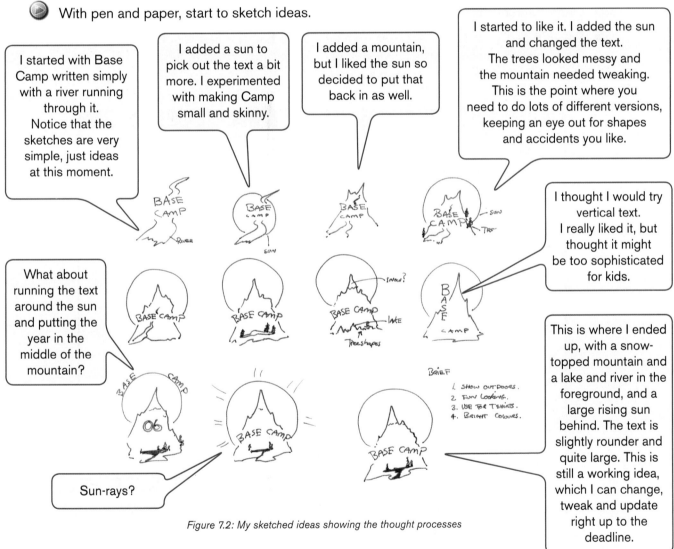

Figure 7.2: My sketched ideas showing the thought processes

For the sample project, you need to show your hand-drawn sketches in the eportfolio. You will need to annotate them and then scan them – or you can scan them, insert them in a Word document and then add annotations. When you come to do the Edexcel SPB, remember to check the Mark Alert pages very carefully to see exactly what evidence you must include for each piece of artwork.

Scanning

Scanning is useful when you need an electronic copy of printed media such as a photo or hand-drawn image. For DiDA, you will probably need to scan images and hand-written notes. For example, if you hand-draw a design for your logo or birthday card, you may need to scan it so that it can be included in your eportfolio, if that is what the SPB specifies.

You can scan an image directly from Fireworks if your scanner is TWAIN compliant (Windows); this is very convenient because you can also edit the scanned image using Fireworks to improve image quality and reduce the file size. To scan from Fireworks:

 Open Macromedia Fireworks.

 Select **File**, **Scan**, **Twain Acquire** from the **Menu** bar. The next window will either be a list from which you need to select your scanner, or it will go directly to the scanner window (if you have scanned from Fireworks before).

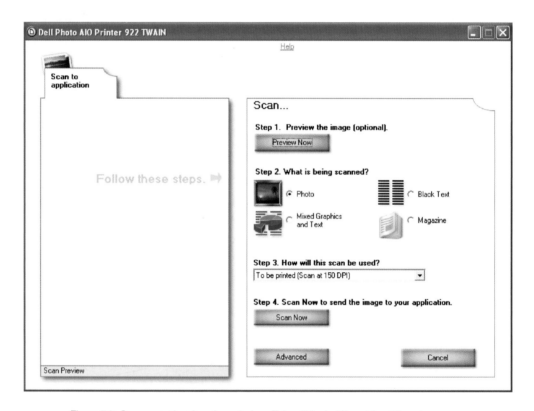

Figure 7.3: Scanner options/preview window. This will look different for different scanners,
but the same options will be available.

Scanned file resolutions

The scanned document will be viewed only on-screen (not printed out) so it will be viewed at **72 pixels/inch** (or dpi). It is worth scanning at a slightly higher resolution than this to ensure that the document is as clear as possible.

When scanning documents for your eportfolio, use a scanning resolution of about **100 pixels/ inch**. Don't be tempted to use a higher resolution than is needed because it will take longer to scan, it will be a larger file and will require more optimization later.

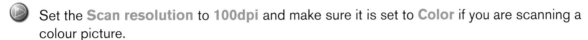 Set the **Scan resolution** to **100dpi** and make sure it is set to **Color** if you are scanning a colour picture.

 Click the **Preview** button to preview what the scan will look like.

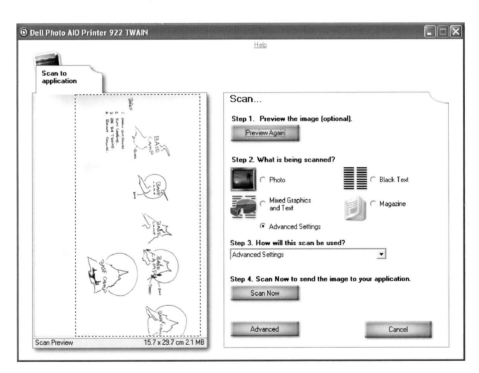

Figure 7.4: Previewing and cropping the scan

If you need only a specific area of the document to be scanned, just click and drag the box in the **Scan Preview** area to surround the part that you want.

Click **Scan** when you're ready.

The scan will take a minute or so, and then the scanned document will appear in the Fireworks workspace.

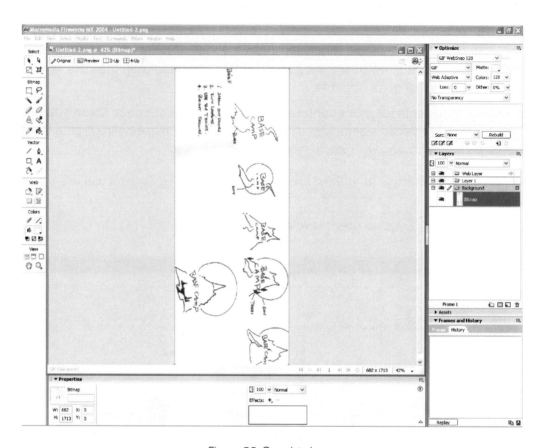

Figures 7.5: Completed scan

 If you need to rotate the image, select Modify, Canvas from the Menu bar. Select a rotate option to suit.

If the scanned document is, say, an A4 page showing a series of sketches to be inserted in your eportfolio, you should resize it now so that you don't have to do it when you insert it into Dreamweaver (it will also make the file size smaller).

 Resize by selecting Modify, Canvas, Image Size from the Menu bar. Enter the width as 700 pixels. This should be large enough so that the sketches are legible, while still fitting into the eportfolio. Press OK to apply the change.

 Save the scanned document by selecting File, Save As from the Menu bar. If you are scanning a set of logo ideas for your eportfolio, you should save it in your Logo\Scans folder. It will be saved as a .png file by default; this is fine as you can save it as a .jpg or .gif file when you optimise it.

Creating the logo

 Create a new canvas with a **Width** of **800 Pixels**, a **Height** of **800 Pixels**, a **Resolution** of **72 Pixels/Inch**, and the **Canvas color** set to **White**.

Using the Pen tool

We will draw the mountain first. You may need to find some pictures of mountains to use as a reference, as this has got to look good.

We will be using the vector **Pen** tool, which is a little tricky to master, so you will need to spend time experimenting with it. Try a test shape first.

 Select the **Pen** tool and match the **Properties inspector** to Figure 7.6.

Pen Icon

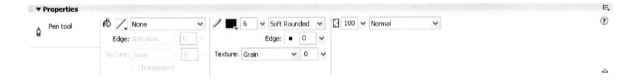

Figure 7.6: Pen tool settings

 First try drawing a closed shape made up of straight lines. Simply click and release the mouse at several points roughly round a square, circle or other shape. When you hover near the first point, you will see a little circle appear to tell you that the next click will close the shape.

 Press the **Delete** key twice to delete your shape.

Now you're ready to try curves – this can be a little tricky at first!

 With the **Pen** tool still selected, click anywhere on the canvas.

 Now position the mouse pointer a short distance away from where you just clicked. This time keep the left button pressed while you drag and then release. A neat curved path appears.

 Repeat. (Position the mouse pointer again a short distance away, then press and hold the left button while you drag and release again.) The beauty of drawing like this is that you can tweak the lines all you want at any stage of the design process.

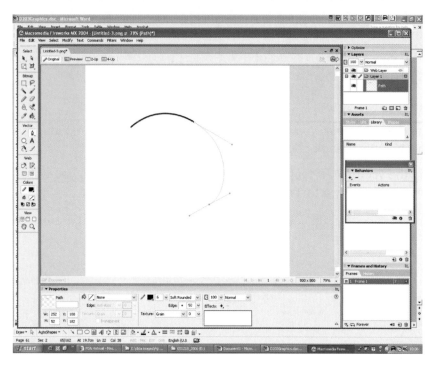

Figure 7.7

Fill color Icon

Stroke color Icon

Subselection Icon

Pointer Icon

Pen Icon

▶ Draw a wobbly line and go all the way back to your original point. Close the shape as before.

▶ In the **Properties inspector**, click on the **Fill color** box and choose a colour to fill your shape with.

▶ Try changing the colour in the **Stroke color** box now. You can even switch it off to leave just the filled shape.

▶ Click the **Subselection** tool and click and drag a point on your shape to move it. You can also delete the selected point by pressing the **Delete** key.

Drawing the mountain shape

▶ That's enough experimenting! With the **Pointer** tool selected, click on your shape and delete it, as we are going to draw the mountain now.

▶ Select the **Pen** tool and make sure the **Properties inspector** looks like Figure 7.6.

▶ Draw the mountain shape using a combination of straight lines and curves. Use the **Subselection** tool to tweak it until you are happy with it. I took nine attempts before I liked mine.

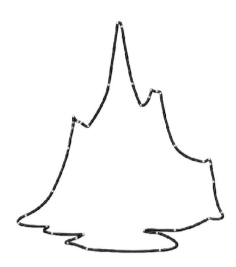

Figure 7.8: The mountain shape

▶ Fill the mountain shape with blue. Look at the **Layers** panel – your mountain shape appears in **Layer 1** with the default name **Path**.

▶ Deselect the mountain by pressing **Crtl-D**.

Drawing the sun

▶ Choose the vector **Ellipse** tool and draw the sun, keeping the **Shift** key pressed to constrain its proportions.

▶ Fill the sun with a warm orangey-yellow and turn off its stroke colour.

Ellipse Icon

In the **Layers** panel, you can order the vector shapes by dragging their object names up or down.

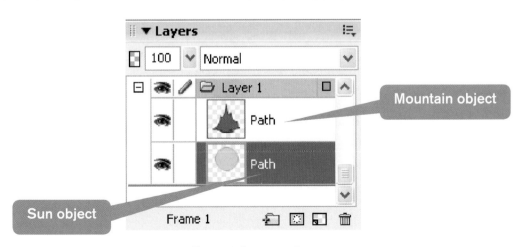

Figure 7.9: Layers panel

- Drag the sun under the mountain in the Layers panel.
- Rename the two objects Mountain and Sun.
- Use Modify, Transform, Free Transform to size and position your circle.

Figure 7.10: Mountain and sun

Snow-capped mountain

- Double-click the name Layer 1 in the Layers panel and rename it MountainAndSun.

*New/Duplicate
Layer Icon*

- Select just the Mountain object and then drag it onto the New/Duplicate Layer icon at the bottom of the Layers panel.

This creates a duplicate of the mountain on a new layer called Layer 1. Rename the layer Snowcap.

- Switch off the MountainAndSun layer by clicking the Eye symbol in the Layers panel. Now all you can see is the duplicate Mountain object.

- Press Ctrl-D to deselect the Mountain object.

Pen Icon

- Select the Pen tool and change the settings in the Properties inspector back to those shown in Figure 7.6.

- Draw a wobbly snowy line, as shown in Figure 7.11. The line needs to show the snowline near the mountain peak. Take the line around the outside of the mountain to close it.

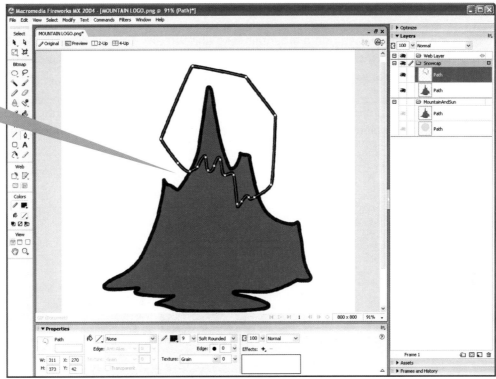

Figure 7.11: Adding a snowy peak

Next we will crop the snow-cap to the exact shape of the mountain peak.

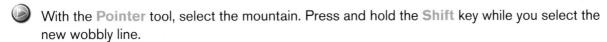 With the **Pointer** tool, select the mountain. Press and hold the **Shift** key while you select the new wobbly line.

From the **Menu** bar, select **Modify**, **Combine Paths**, **Crop**. We now have our snow shape!

Figure 7.12

Change the **Fill** colour to white.

Switch on the **MountainAndSun** layer.

Lake and stream

 Now see if you can add a mountain lake and stream. You will need to make a new layer with the **Mountain** object on it, exactly as before, and name the layer **LakeAndStream**. Use the **Pen** tool to draw a lake and stream, and crop as before.

The final tweaks are up to you. Use the **Pointer** tool to select the separate shapes and then change the **Fill** colours and the **Stroke** sizes and colours to make a punchy image.

Figure 7.13: All coloured up!

Using the Text tool

Adding the text is the 'make or break' moment for this logo – we need to make sure it is readable, fun and looks good.

Your computer probably has many different typefaces, so spend some time exploring them. When you select one, remember who the logo is designed to appeal to and what the logo will be used for.

First we need a new layer. This keeps our artwork neat and organised; when you are working on a much more complicated piece of artwork, this will be even more necessary!

New/Duplicate Layer Icon

 Click the **New/Duplicate Layer** icon.

 Rename the layer **TitleText**.

Text Icon

 Click on the **Text** tool in the **Vector** section of the **Tools** panel.

In the **Properties inspector**, make sure the text is left-aligned, and select a suitable font (**Comic Sans MS** will do) about size **60**, in a green colour.

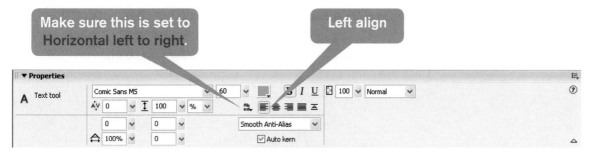

Figure 7.14: The Text tool settings

Click on the canvas. You will notice that Fireworks has made a new vector object called **Text** in the **TitleText** layer.

Type **Base Camp**.

To move the text, you must first select it with the **Pointer** tool. Do this, and then play with the colours and typefaces. You could try adding an effect or two. (Click the **+** sign next to **Filters** (**Effects** in Fireworks MX).

For your eportfolio, you could save two or three versions with different text styles. Check first if you are required to show early versions.

For now, choose the best version and we will finish off the logo.

Attaching text to a path

The logo probably looks OK at the moment, but we will give the text a curve to see if that makes it look even better.

Draw a large vector **Ellipse**, and in the **Properties inspector** set the fill to **None** and make a **1** pixel **black** stroke.

Press **Shift** and select the text.

From the **Menu** bar, choose **Text**, **Attach to Path**.

Ellipse Icon

Figure 7.15: Attaching text to a path

● Click the **Text** tool and click on the ellipse in front of the **Base Camp** text – you may need to add some spaces to centralise the text.

● Save this version of the logo and then add some tweaks and colour changes until it is perfect.

● Save the final version as **BaseCampLogo.png** in the **Logo\Artwork** folder.

Figure 7.16: The finished logo

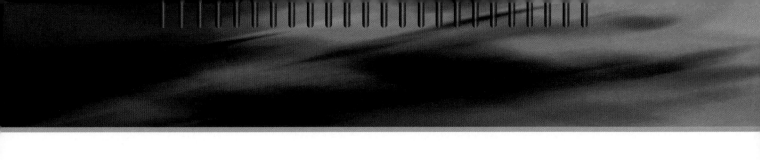

Good Marks... ✓

You will get good marks if:

- you show how you developed your design
- you use vector graphics so the logo can be scaled up or down without losing any detail
- you use at least three different colours
- your logo looks effective in different sizes
- your logo looks effective in both colour and monochrome
- you use the logo in other artworks for this project
- you have asked test users for feedback
- you have made changes where necessary
- you have recorded all images in your Elements table.

Bad Marks... ✗

You will lose marks if:

- you use clip art or WordArt unnecessarily
- your logo is overly complex or detailed
- it is not suitable for the type of organization, or the age group it is designed to appeal to.

You can create some spectacular results very quickly by adding different filters or effects to a picture. You can also transform a photograph into something quite different! We have already used effects such as drop shadows and a little bit of moulding on vector shapes.

In this chapter you will create a fancy button to use in your eportfolio, and you'll be adding special effects to two different photographs. These could be placed in your Base Camp web page or used on postcards, birthday cards, brochures or posters.

Brushed steel button

 Create a new canvas with a **Width** of **500 Pixels**, a **Height** of **500 Pixels**, a **Resolution** of **72 Pixels/Inch**, and the **Canvas color** set to **Transparent**.

New Bitmap Icon

 Click the **New Bitmap Image** icon at the bottom of the **Layers** panel; this will give us a transparent canvas to work on.

Select the **Paint Bucket** tool, choose a light grey, and flood the canvas with the colour.

On the **Menu** bar, choose **Filters**, **Noise**, **Add Noise**, and match the **Add Noise** window to Figure 8.1. Press **OK**.

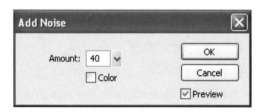

Figure 8.1: Adding noise

 Choose **Filters**, **Blur**, **Motion Blur**, and match the direction and length of the blur to Figure 8.2: Angle **0** and Distance **38**. Press **OK**.

Figure 8.2: Motion Blur

There are several ways to do the next stage, but the method explained below is the best because it is the easiest to update.

 Select the **Oval Marquee** tool and check that the **Edge** property is set to **Anti-alias**. Draw a circle selection on the stainless steel background.

Oval Marquee Icon

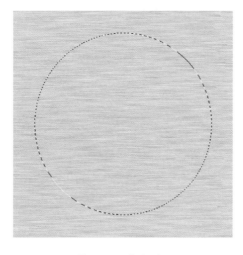

Figure 8.3: Selection

 From the **Menu** bar, choose **Select**, **Select Inverse** to select everything *except* the current selection. Press the **Delete** key to clear the unwanted background.

 Press **Ctrl-D** to deselect. In the **Layers** panel, rename this layer (**Layer 1**) as **Button**. (Double-click the layer name to do this.)

 Drag the **Button** layer down onto the **New/Duplicate Layer** icon to duplicate this layer.

New/Duplicate Icon

 Rename the new layer **ButtonCopy**.

 Click on the **Pointer** tool, which should automatically select the **ButtonCopy** layer. Click on your newly-drawn button and, in the **Properties inspector**, press the **Add live filters** button and choose **Candy 4000 LE**, **Bevel Boss**. (In Fireworks MX, it is called the **Add effects** button.)

Add Live Filters Icon

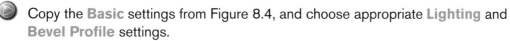 Copy the **Basic** settings from Figure 8.4, and choose appropriate **Lighting** and **Bevel Profile** settings.

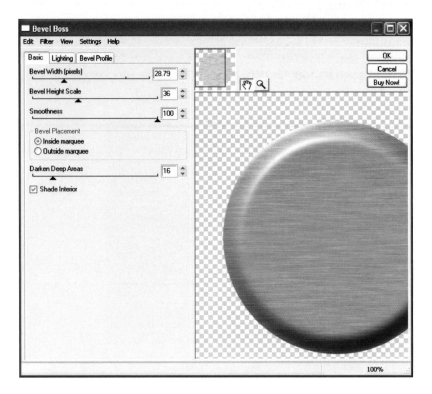

Figure 8.4: Bevel Boss

 Click **OK**.

 Find the vector shape **Arrow** (it shares a spot in the **Tools** panel with the **Rectangle** tool and **Ellipse** tool).

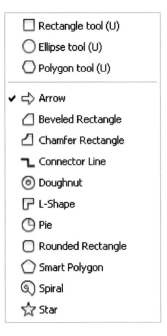

Figure 8.5: Vector tools

Draw an arrow onto the button. Have a play with the various nodes around the arrow path – the blue nodes change the size of the arrow and the yellow ones change the shape. Experiment and you will find there are a few surprises!

Figure 8.6: Adding the arrow

With the arrow still selected, from the **Properties inspector** add a new filter by clicking the **Add live filters** button (**Add effects** in Fireworks MX), and this time choose **Adjust Color, Hue/Saturation**. Use the settings shown in Figure 8.7.

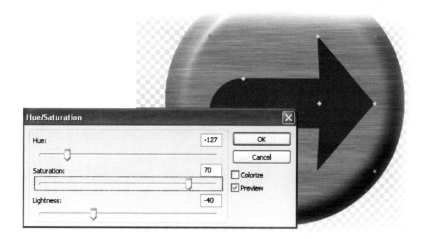

Figure 8.7: Hue/Saturation

The next bit is up to you! Add a **bevel** and a **drop shadow** filter, to make the button look as stylish as possible. We are going to use it in the eportfolio later.

Lastly we need a shadow for the button itself, which we can make by using an effect.

Turn off the **Button Copy** layer to reveal the **Button** layer. We'll make this layer into the shadow. Select the circle and, from the **Menu** bar, select **Filters, Adjust Color, Brightness/Contrast**. Make your stainless steel go black and press **OK**.

Eye Icon

75

You will notice that in the **Properties inspector** there is no option to switch off or change the filter, although it is not uncommon to have to do this!

Now go to **Filters**, **Blur**, **Gaussian Blur**. Set it to about **10** and press **OK.**

Eye Icon

Switch the **Button copy layer** on and marvel at your home-made drop shadow. Using the **Pointer** tool, move the **Button** layer to get the shadow in the perfect place, matching the shadow with the highlights on your arrow.

Now click again on the arrow. You can see all your **Filters** are still attached, and if you want to tweak the colour just click on the **Edit and arrange live filters** button next to **Hue/Saturation** (see Figure 8.8).

Have a look at real objects and note how light shines on one side and the shadow falls on the other side!

The Edit and arrange live filters button

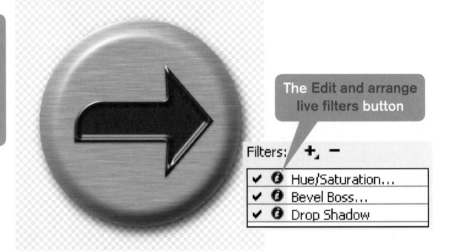

Filters: **+** **−**

✔ *i* Hue/Saturation...
✔ *i* Bevel Boss...
✔ *i* Drop Shadow

Figure 8.8: Editing your filters

Save your button in the **Components** folder as **Button.png**, and close the file.

Don't forget to make an entry for it in your **Elements** table.

! Tip:

When you scale an image that has live filters, you will almost certainly need to update the settings.

Downloading photographs for the sample project

For the next two exercises, you will need to download photographs from the Payne-Gallway website. All the images you need for this sample project are on the Payne-Gallway website: **www.payne-gallway.co.uk**.

 Go to the website and follow the links to download the images for D203. Save them in your **DownloadedImages** folder.

Adding the Wow factor

Most of my work involves making photographs better or more exciting; this is one brilliant way of giving some wow factor.

Experimenting with layer blend modes can sometimes bring up some nice accidents. It is impossible sometimes to sketch ideas before you try to make an artwork, so try to make sure you save versions of your artwork as you get closer to finishing it. Every time I make a step forwards or I see something I like, I save straightaway using the picture name followed by **V1**, **V2** and so on (for Version 1, Version 2). That way I can always go back to a previous version if the next hour's work doesn't turn out well.

 Load Fireworks if it is not already open.

 From the **Menu** bar, select **File**, **Open** and browse to find your **DownloadedImages** folder. Change the **Files of type** box to **JPEG**.

 Select the picture **CatamaranSailing.jpg** and click **Open**.

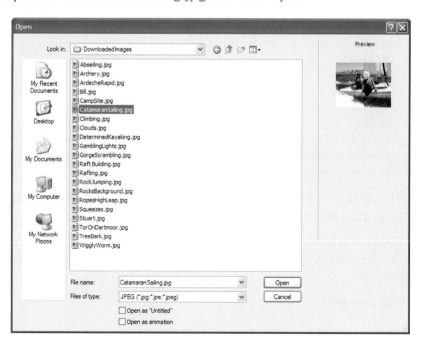

Figure 8.9: Loading a JPEG file

Oval Marquee Icon

Choose the **Oval Marquee** tool, and in the **Properties inspector** check that the **Style** is **Normal** and **Edge** is set to **Feather 100**. Feathering the selection makes the edge blurred.

Draw an oval selection around the sailors, as shown in Figure 8.8.

Figure 8.10: Feathered selection

Paint Bucket Icon

You can see how your selection looks by using the **Paint Bucket** tool, setting the **Opacity** to **100**, and choosing a colour to show up against the photo. Tick the **Fill selection** box. Click in the middle of the selection.

Press **Ctrl-Z** to undo the fill. We want to apply a filter to the outside of the selection, so go to the **Menu** bar and choose **Select, Select Inverse**.

Now select **Filters, Blur, Zoom Blur**. I decided to set the options at **Amount 30** and **Quality 80**. It might take a few moments to apply the filter, depending on the speed of your computer. Press **OK**.

Press **Ctrl-D** to deselect!

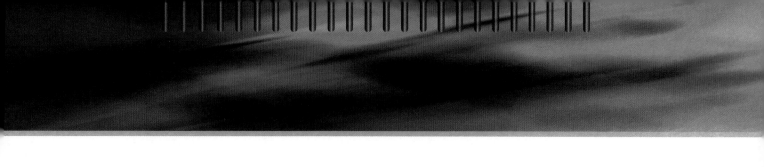

Figure 8.11: Zoooom!

Well, that gives the picture wow factor! We can now add some spectacular colour changes by adding another effect.

 Save the picture in the **D203Exercises** folder.

 At the top right of the **Layers** panel, you will find the **Options** button – click it and choose **Duplicate layer**, click the **After current layer** button and then click **OK**.

 Select both of the layers. At the top of the **Layers** panel, change the **Blend modes**, and experiment to see how different blends work to make some very stylish and some very bad results.

Options Icon

Figure 8.12: Layer Blend modes

New Bitmap Icon

 Add a **New Bitmap Image** and add some filled shapes, then use the blend options in the **Layers** panel to make a surreal coloured creation… can you do better than mine?

Figure 8.13: Wow… hand me a pair of sunglasses!

 Save your favourite version in the **D203Exercises** folder.

Background image

Sometimes a filtered photograph can be used as a background for text. You have to remember that the text needs to be legible, so the colours you use are very important if the message is to come across clearly.

A background which is basically black or dark grey looks cool and classy, and yellow or grey will look more sporty or can be used for a warning sign.

Consider whether your design needs to grab people's attention. If it does, what age group is it aimed at? Could you use an image of a famous footballer or pop group, or use shock tactics to get people to look and read? (This would not be applicable or desirable for the Base Camp brochure!)

I have used the techniques described in this next exercise several times. They can be used with photographic images that are not particularly crisp, as long as they have good colour contrast, so that the shapes can be picked out clearly.

 Load the picture **CampSite.jpg** from your **DownloadedImages** folder.

Figure 8.14: Camp site   © Acorn Adventure

At the bottom of the photograph there is a canoe and fire-fighting equipment.

 Use the **Rubber Stamp** tool to clone some gravel and paint them out. Choose your brush size carefully, and you might want to drop the opacity down to **75**. (Look back at Chapter 4 if you can't remember how to use the **Rubber Stamp** tool.)

Rubber Stamp Icon

Figure 8.15: Gone!

As you can see, the photo is a bit blurred but has lots of contrast, and we can try out a combination of effects that will work well with this image.

 Pick the **Pointer** tool and click on the canvas. Click on the **Add live filters** button and select **Other**, **Find Edges**.

The image is not very usable like this, but something I like to try with my images is to invert them, so that black becomes white and vice versa.

 Click on the **Add live filters** button (**Add effects** in Fireworks MX) and select **Adjust Color**, **Invert**.

Figure 8.16: Inverted, it looks like a pencil sketch!

Now we can colour it. We could use another layer with a colour, and use a **Layer Blend mode** so that the camp site is visible too, but this time we will add another effect to change and customise the background.

Add live filters Icon

Click the **Add live filters** button and go to **Adjust Color**, **Hue/Saturation**. Copy the settings from Figure 8.17 and make sure you tick the **Colorize** checkbox. Press **OK** to apply the change.

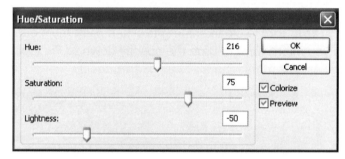

Figure 8.17: Settings for the colorized background

Figure 8.18: Coloured background

You could now add, say, white text to this coloured background.

Important Note:

Remember that all you need to do is click the **Edit and arrange live filters** icon in the **Properties inspector** to update the image. The original picture is untouched, and if you switch off all the filters you can see it.

Edit and arrange live filters Icon

 From the **Menu** bar, select **File**, **Save**.

A message will be displayed telling you that you must save this as a **PNG** file if you want to be able to edit it further.

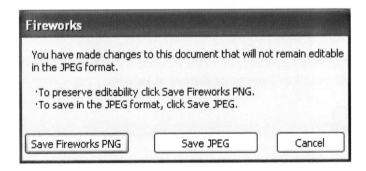

Figure 8.19

 Click **Save Fireworks PNG**. Save the file in your **D203Exercises** folder.

 Close the file.

In this chapter you will learn how to use a grid and guides so that you can accurately lay out a folded document, such as a brochure or birthday card. If you had to produce a brochure, you would probably use desktop publishing software, but you could use Fireworks to create some text headings and graphics to use in the brochure. These would then be reusable in future brochures.

We will take a closer look at how to create and edit text, and the options you can use to change its appearance in different ways.

Laying out a grid

For the brochure, I chose the size of the canvas to be roughly A3 size, assuming that the finished brochure will be an A3 sheet folded in the middle.

Important Note:

72dpi is not a sufficiently high resolution for printed material. Therefore, this is strictly a mock-up which will be viewed only on-screen.

 Create a new canvas with a **Width** of **1200 Pixels**, a **Height** of **850 Pixels**, a **Resolution** of **72 Pixels/Inch**, and the **Canvas color** set to **White**.

 Tip:

You can calculate the physical size of the canvas in inches by dividing the number of pixels by the resolution in pixels/dots per inch. Therefore this canvas will be 1200 ÷ 72 = 16.7 inches wide and 850 ÷ 72 = 11.8 inches tall, which is roughly the size of an A3 sheet in landscape orientation.

 Go to **View** on the **Menu** bar, and choose **Grid**, **Show Grid**. The screen is now covered in squares, but the grid needs to be edited for our purposes.

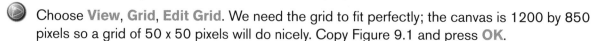 Choose **View**, **Grid**, **Edit Grid**. We need the grid to fit perfectly; the canvas is 1200 by 850 pixels so a grid of 50 x 50 pixels will do nicely. Copy Figure 9.1 and press **OK**.

Important Note:

Notice that **Snap to grid** is checked – this will ensure that objects are placed exactly on gridlines rather than just very close to them.

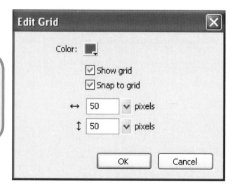

Figure 9.1: Setting the grid

Next it will be useful to have rulers so we can find the middle of the canvas and pull out guides to mark out the layout.

 Select **View**, **Rulers**.

 Now select **View**, **Guides**, **Edit Guides**, copy Figure 9.2 and choose a dark red colour for the guides. Press **OK** to apply the changes.

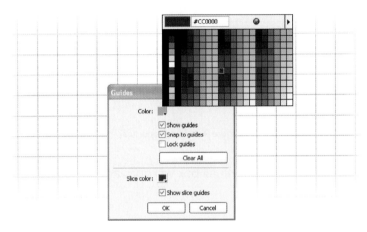

Figure 9.2: Editing the guides

 Tip:

If you are working on a dark canvas, you will need to choose light colours so you can see your grid and guides.

 Press **Ctrl-0** (that's **Ctrl** and **zero**, the shortcut key combination for **Fit All**). This will fit all of your canvas onto the screen.

 Click and hold on the left-hand ruler, drag a guide and measure along the top ruler **600 pixels**.

 Look at Figure 9.3, and draw out guides so you have two pages marked out ready to design your brochure.

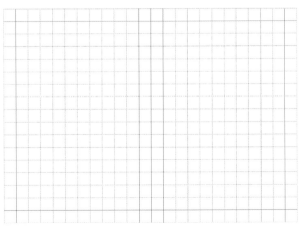

Figure 9.3: Grid and guides

Adding text

Next we will add some text and position it carefully.

A

Text Icon

▶ Pick the **Text** tool and set the properties as shown in Figure 9.4. If you have not got the **Alba** font, choose something else.

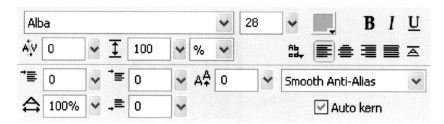

Figure 9.4: Text Properties

▶ Click somewhere on the canvas. A small box will appear and you can start typing.

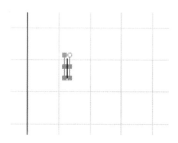

Figure 9.5

▶ Type **BASE CAMP (Enter) The best fun you will ever have!**

▶ Use the **Pointer** tool to position the text on the top left of the grid, and stretch the text box over to the right-hand guide.

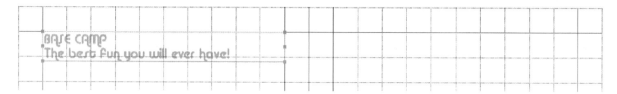

Figure 9.6: Text moved into position

Editing text

You can edit and manipulate text in the **Text Editor** dialogue box. You can display this by selecting **Text**, **Editor** from the **Menu** bar, or by double-clicking the **Text** tool while your text box is selected.

Text Icon

 Display the **Text Editor** dialogue box.

Figure 9.7: Text editor

 Try selecting the title and making it much larger.

Scaling text

 Experiment with different typefaces. Try selecting the second line and clicking the **Stretched alignment** button so the text fits right across the text space. Press **OK** when you have finished.

Stretched alignment Icon

Vertical text

Suppose you wanted to have vertical text down the left margin of the second page.

 Make sure nothing is currently selected.

 Click the **Text** tool. In the **Properties inspector**, click the button to the left of the **Text alignment** buttons. Choose **Vertical left to right**.

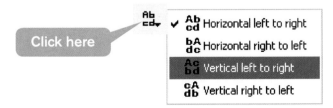

Figure 9.8

▶ Type **Base Camp** on the second page.

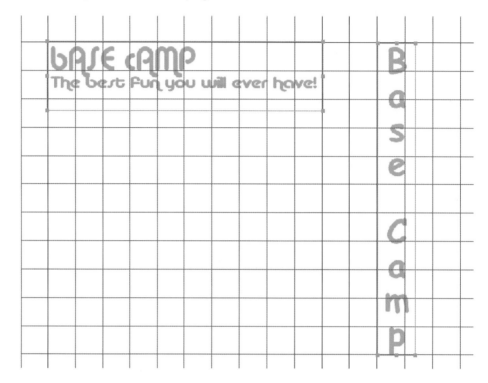

Figure 9.9

▶ Save your work as **BrochureInside.png** in your **D203Exercises** folder, and close it.

Combining text and effects

The next piece of artwork we will create will be a sign for Base Camp using a wood effect so that it looks as if the letters have been burned onto a piece of wood. We will use Fireworks textured fills and effects to achieve this.

▶ Create a new canvas with a **Width** of **500 Pixels**, a **Height** of **350 Pixels**, a **Resolution** of **72 Pixels/Inch**, and the **Canvas color** set to **White**.

Text Icon

▶ Select the **Text** tool and, in the **Properties inspector**, make sure that the **Stretch Alignment** button is not selected, that **text orientation** is set to **Horizontal left to right**, and the text is centred. The colour is not important – leave it as green.

▶ Choose a typeface that suggests a home-made sign and enter a large font size, say **120**. (You will need to type in the font size, rather than using the slider, to get it big enough to nicely fill the whole canvas.)

▶ Click towards the middle of the canvas and type **Base** (**Enter**) **Camp**.

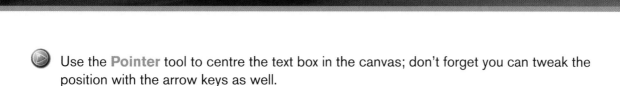

Use the **Pointer** tool to centre the text box in the canvas; don't forget you can tweak the position with the arrow keys as well.

With the **Pointer** tool or the **Text** tool selected, click the **Color** box in the **Properties inspector**, as we are going to explore the **Fill options**.

Pointer Icon

Click **Fill Options** at the bottom of the **Color** pop-up window, find the **Fill category** at the top of the **Fill options** and change it to **Pattern**.

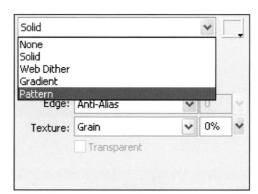

Figure 9.10: Pattern

Click the **Pattern name** and scroll down to find **Wood**.

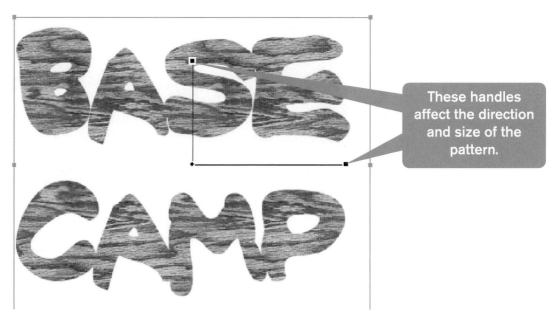

These handles affect the direction and size of the pattern.

Figure 9.11: Wood fill

This next bit is up to you. It will take a bit of work, so really try to achieve the right effect: the lettering has to appear as if it is engraved, or carved, into the background.

 Add a **live filter** – you can use **Bevel and Emboss**, **Inset Emboss** or the **Eye Candy 4000 LE**, **Bevel Boss**.

 With the vector **Rectangle** tool, draw a rectangle over the entire canvas. It should fill automatically with the **wood** pattern. If it is does not, fill it using options in the **Properties inspector**.

Rectangle Icon

In the **Layers** panel, drag the **Rectangle** object under the **Text** object.

 Select the **Text** object.

 Add another **live filter**. Select **Adjust Color**, **Hue/Saturation**, and make the text look burnt by darkening it and taking a little colour saturation out – have a look at Figure 9.12 for reference.

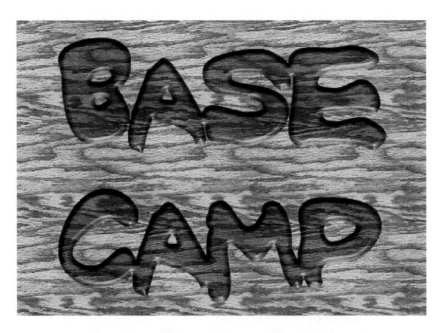

Figure 9.12: Wood background

 To add some realism, add one more **live filter**. Choose **Shadow and Glow**, **Glow**, change the colour to a dark brown; tweak the **Softness**, **Width** and **Opacity** to make a soft burnt feel around the letters.

Figure 9.13: Finished wood sign

Save your sign as **WoodSign.png** in the **D203Exercises** folder.

If one of the Base Camp campers has a birthday, we need to have some cards ready! Let's create a card using the Base Camp Bunny.

Preparation work for the eportfolio

The design for a birthday card is one of the pieces of artwork you will include in your eportfolio for the sample SPB. For this piece of work, you are also required to make a hand-drawn mock-up of the real card, photograph it and include this as evidence of your design. Also, you must show the dimensions and scale of the card and show how you used a grid to ensure the picture was correctly positioned on the front of the card. Finally, you must show the finished version of the outside of the card.

Making a mock-up of the card

Remember that this card is for kids, so it has to be bright and bold. It will have a front and back, and it will have some text inside (but you do not have to show this in the sample eportfolio).

I measured some birthday cards and found that 18 cm high and 14 cm wide (28 cm wide opened out) seems a good average. This will fit on an A4 page, so it can easily be printed out.

Think about where the front of the card will be when it is laid flat. It would be a good idea to make a mock-up of the card, to make sure you don't mess up. A trip to an advertising agency will reveal mocks-ups of all sorts of products in cardboard or paper form. Even the professionals need to look at and handle a physical object – quite often this will spark an idea or two – at the very least, it will help them to understand what they are dealing with.

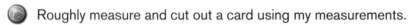 Roughly measure and cut out a card using my measurements.

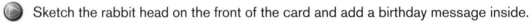 Sketch the rabbit head on the front of the card and add a birthday message inside.

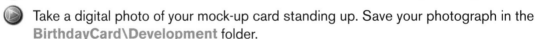 Take a digital photo of your mock-up card standing up. Save your photograph in the **BirthdayCard\Development** folder.

Figure 10.1: My card

Modifying the canvas size

▶ Open **BaseCampBunny3d.png**.

▶ Save the file as **RabbitCardV1** in **BirthdayCard\Artwork**.

We will create the card artwork at 72dpi (screen resolution). As it will be vector art, we can enlarge it for print later without affecting the quality.

▶ Go to **Modify**, **Canvas**, **Image size**, check the resolution is set to **72dpi** and press **OK**.

▶ Next choose **Modify**, **Canvas**, **Canvas size**, change **pixels** to **centimeters** and make the size **28 cm** wide and **18 cm** high. Press **OK**.

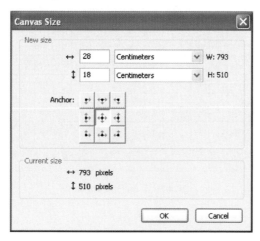

Figure 10.2: Changing the canvas size

Show/Hide Icon

The rabbit will probably not fit on the canvas – don't panic! We will fix this shortly.

In the **Layers** panel, rename **Layer 1** as **BaseCampBunny**.

Let's hide the rabbit while we set up the grid. First, press the little – sign on the **BaseCampBunny** layer to collapse all the objects in the layer. Then press the **Show/Hide** icon (in the shape of an eye) to hide the rabbit.

Editing and displaying the grid

The grid needs to be switched on and edited, so we can measure out the card with guides. Click **Modify**, **Canvas**, **Canvas Size**, and round the number of pixels so it can be divided by **20**. I made my card **800** wide and **500** high. Click **OK**.

Now select **View**, **Grid**, **Edit Grid**. Edit your grid so you have squares of **20 pixels**. If the grid is not displayed, click **View**, **Grid**, **Show Grid**.

Make sure the rulers and guides are displayed and mark out your card with guides (see Figure 10.3).

Tip:

You can drag the crosshairs at the intersection of the ruler lines to line up the zero position of the horizontal and vertical rulers with the top left corner of the card.

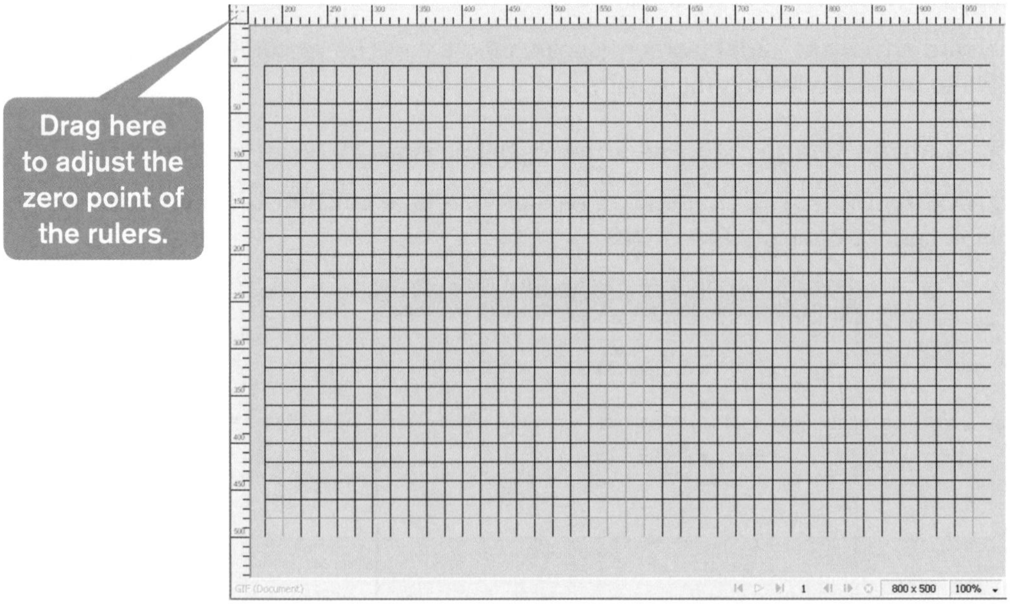

Drag here to adjust the zero point of the rulers.

Figure 10.3: Marked-out card

Scaling the vector drawing

▶ Switch the **Base Camp Bunny** layer back on.

▶ **Zoom out** so you can see the entire bunny.

▶ With the **Pointer** tool, drag a selection right across the bunny.

▶ Pick the **Scale** tool in the **Tools** panel and scale the bunny head down so it fits on the right-hand page, using the guides to get the head nice and central.

Scale Tool Icon

> **Tip:**
>
> Press **Ctrl-Space** to zoom in and **Ctrl-Alt-Space** to zoom out if you need to.

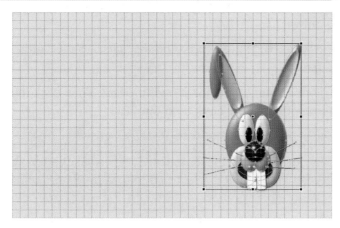

Figure 10.4: Positioning Base Camp Bunny

▶ Save the card again as **RabbitCardV1** in **BirthdayCard\Artwork**.

Taking a screenshot

A great tip for recording your stages of your work is to use screen grabs. You can take screenshots of anything from Internet sites to a computer game, and edit or crop them in Fireworks. We'll take a screenshot of the canvas with its rulers and guides, and save it in **BirthdayCard\Development** for later insertion in the eportfolio.

▶ If you cannot see the whole canvas on the screen, click the **Zoom** tool, right-click on your canvas and choose **Fit All** (or press **Ctrl-0**).

Zoom Tool Icon

▶ Press the **Print Screen** key, usually found at top right on your keyboard.

▶ From the **Menu** bar, select **File**, **New**, and press **OK** as Fireworks has already changed the canvas size ready for the screenshot.

▶ Right-click and **Fit All** again.

▶ Press **Ctrl-V** to paste (or select **Edit**, **Paste**).

▶ You may need to turn off the grid and guides so that you can see your screenshot more clearly.

Crop Tool Icon

▶ You will have captured and pasted the entire screen, so choose the **Crop** tool and drag a crop box over the part you want to keep. You can edit the size of the box by moving the black nodes. Press **Enter** when you're done.

▶ Save your screen grab as **RabbitAndGrid.png** in **BirthdayCard\Development**.

▶ You can close this file now, and we will continue with the birthday card. If you turned off the grid and guides, turn them on again now.

Adding text

▶ Make a new layer and name it **Circle**. Drag the new layer underneath the **BaseCampBunny** layer.

▶ Draw a big red circle on the **Circle** layer using the vector **Ellipse** tool, keeping **Shift** pressed while you draw it.

▶ Use the **Text** tool to write **Happy Birthday** on this layer. We will attach it to the circular path in the next step.

▶ Draw another, smaller circle and position it over the first. Then click the **Pointer** tool, and press **Shift** to select both the new circle and the text.

▶ From the **Menu** bar, select **Text, Attach to Path**.

▶ Double-click the **Text** tool and use the **Text Editor** to tweak the text. When you are satisfied with the first **Happy Birthday**, edit the text to add a second one running round the bottom of the circle.

▶ You may need to scale the bunny again to get the text to fit nicely around him.

Figure 10.5: Attach to Path

▶ I added a **Radial blur** from the **Live filters** to give the text a bit of movement – be very careful that you can still read it.

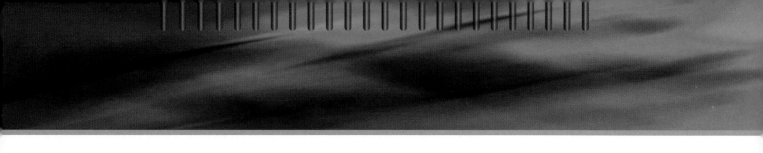

Adding a text background

To finish off the front and back of the card, we can make a background composed entirely of text. We will start by positioning the text on the left-hand page.

 Make a new layer, and call it **TextBackground**. Drag the new layer so that it is underneath the other two layers.

 Write **BASE CAMP** three times in a fairly small (say, 16 point) grey font.

 Use the **Pointer** tool to position the text inside the guides.

Figure 10.6: Positioning the text box

 With the new text selected, double-click the **Text** tool icon in the **Tools** panel; use the **Stretched Alignment** button to stretch the text across the text box.

 Press **OK**.

Next we need to select the text and copy and paste it so we get a block of text.

 Make sure the background text is selected and double-click the **Text** tool.

 The **BASE CAMP** text will be selected so press **Ctrl-C** to copy the text, click at the end of the text and press **Enter**. Press **Ctrl-V** to paste the text. Press **Enter** and **Ctrl-V** again, and repeat until you have a page of text. Press **OK** to confirm the change.

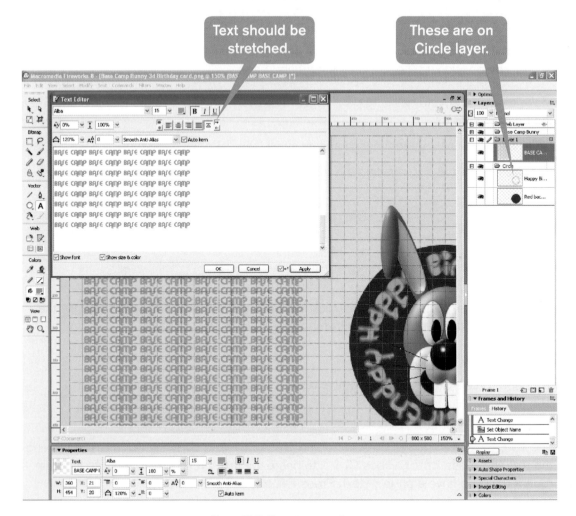

Figure 10.7: Repeat copy and paste

🔘 In the **Layers** panel, click on the **Text** object in the **TextBackground** layer, and drag it onto the **New Bitmap Image** icon to clone the text.

🔘 Use the **Pointer** tool to drag the text over to the right page, keeping the **Shift** key pressed to lock the text into a horizontal plane.

🔘 Change the canvas colour to a colour of your choice by going to the **Menu** bar and selecting **Modify**, **Canvas**, **Canvas Color**. (Tip: How about using one of the 'corporate colours' from the logo?)

🔘 This is a good moment to adjust colours and make tweaks to your card. You could add a logo to the back of the card.

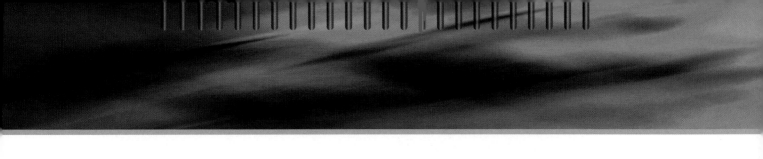

Figure 10.8: Card with background

● This bit is up to you! If you want to put some text on the inside of your card, make a **New Layer**. Call it **InsideCardText**.

● Hide your other layers but keep the guides.

● Add a birthday greeting from the Base Camp staff and kids!

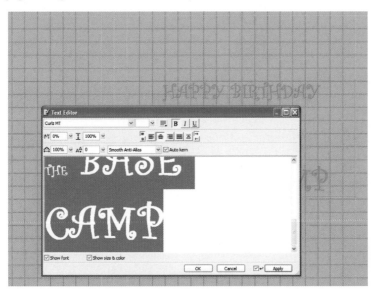

Figure 10.9: Birthday greeting

● Save the final version with a new name in **BirthdayCard\Artwork**.

Good Marks... ✓

You will get good marks if you:

- make a mock-up of your card and show a photograph of it
- show the dimensions of your card
- show how you laid out the card accurately using a grid and/or guidelines
- design a card that is appropriate for an age group that Base Camp caters for
- make the card clearly identifiable as a Base Camp birthday card
- show the front and back of the final card
- ask for feedback and show any changes that you made in response to feedback
- keep a record in the **Elements** table of all images used or created.

Bad Marks... ✗

You will lose marks if you:

- wrongly position the front of the card
- do not use any original artwork
- include features that are not suitable for a printed card.

Chapter 11 – Creating a Postcard

In this chapter we will look at how to put text onto two different photographs to make postcards which could be sold at Base Camp.

When graphic artists produce artwork for a project like this, they have to think of ideas that will strengthen the brand – in this case the Base Camp, an activity centre for 9–14 year-olds. Branding can be achieved in many ways; for example by using a logo, a colour scheme, a font or a particular image. Think of McDonald's – the logo is the big M, the colour scheme is red and yellow, the font is very distinctive and a key figure is Ronald McDonald the clown.

We have already created a logo, which uses the colours blue, yellow and green. We have Base Camp Bunny as a kind of mascot. If this is used over and over, it will make people think of Base Camp whenever they see it. We have also used a particular typeface throughout. Any publicity material we produce should use the corporate colours, the corporate typeface, and display the logo, the mascot, or both.

The postcards will be sent to friends outside the camp, and we can use them to advertise the camp by making it look like a fun place to be. Adding a logo and using the Base Camp colours and typeface will help to strengthen the brand and keep it in people's minds.

You can add messages to persuade people that Base Camp is a fantastic place to go and have fun – you must try to sell this idea with pictures, snappy tag lines and text.

Let's start the postcard.

 Open picture **Abseiling.jpg** which you should already have downloaded from **www.payne-gallway.co.uk** to your **DownloadedImages** folder. If you can't see it, set the **Files of type** box to **All readable files**.

Figure 11.1: Abseiling   © *Acorn Adventure*

 Turn off the grid (if it is still on) by clicking **View**, **Grid** and deselecting **Show Grid**.

Painting the logo on the rocks

The first stage is to add the logo. To add a touch of originality, we can make it look as though it has been painted onto the rock face.

- Open your last version of the Base Camp logo.

- In the **Layers** panel, select each object by holding down **Ctrl** and left-clicking each object (on every layer) in turn. This will select all of your vector shapes.

- Go to **Modify**, **Group**. Your Base Camp logo is now ready to be moved in one grouped vector shape.

- Press **Ctrl-C** to copy the logo. Click the **Abseiling.jpg** tab at the top of your canvas.

- Make a new layer and call it **BaseCampLogo**.

- Press **Ctrl-V** to paste the logo into your new layer.

- With the Base Camp logo selected, go to **Modify**, **Transform**, **Distort**. Move the black nodes to make the logo look natural on the rocks – look at Figure 11.2 for reference.

Figure 11.2: Distorting the logo

- At the top of the **Layers** panel, change the **Blend mode** from **Normal** to **Overlay** to blend the logo into the rock! (See Figure 11.3.)

Tip:

If you are using Fireworks MX, reduce the opacity of the logo, as there is no **Overlay** blend.

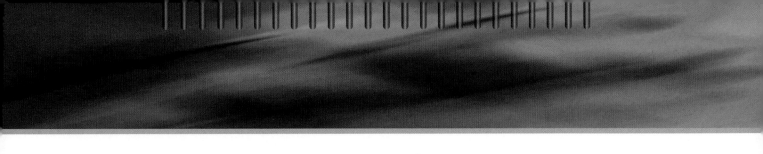

Colour sampling

▶ Make a new layer and call it **Message**.

▶ Use the vector **Rectangle** tool to draw a rectangle on the right-hand side.

We will fill the rectangle with a colour from the logo. We need to sample the colour to make sure it is an identical colour. We can get the colour in several ways; here is one of them.

▶ Change the **Blend mode** of the **Base Camp Logo** layer back to **Normal**.

▶ Now select the rectangle either by using the **Pointer** tool or by clicking on its thumbnail in the **Layers** panel.

▶ Click on the **Fill color box** in the **Properties inspector** and move the eyedropper icon over to the logo, then click on the colour you want to sample. I chose a blue because I felt it made the sky look even bigger and didn't detract from the impact of the image.

Final touches

▶ Next add some text. Think of something witty to say. Use the same or similar typeface and colours as your logo; this will help tie your products together and give them a coherent look.

▶ Redo the **Blend mode** of the logo.

▶ Save your file as **AbseilingPostcard.png** in your **D203Exercises** folder. Close the file, but leave the **BaseCampLogo** file open.

Figure 11.3: Finished postcard

Creating a feeling of movement

Some campers might prefer a postcard like the one shown in Figure 11.4; we can create an impression of high-octane action.

 Open the image **RockJumping.jpg**.

We need to make a copy of the layer because the blur filter that we are going to apply sometimes makes the canvas edges transparent.

New Bitmap Image Icon

Drag the **Bitmap** thumbnail image onto the **New Bitmap Image** icon in the **Layers** panel.

Make sure the top **Bitmap** is selected, then apply a **live filter**: **Blur**, **Radial Blur**. Not too much – look at mine in Figure 11.4.

Figure 11.4: Radial blur   © *Acorn Adventure*

Save the file as **RockJump.png** in the **D203Exercises** folder.

Adding custom colours to the Swatches panel

We will add some text and graphics to this image, and we want them to use the same colours as are used in the logo. We can add all the colours from the logo to the **Swatches** panel so that whatever graphic we are working on, they will always be handy.

Click the **BaseCampLogo.png** tab, or open the file if it isn't already open.

With the logo in front of you, open the **Colors** panel. You can do this by selecting **Window**, **Color Mixer** from the **Menu** bar.

In the **Colors** panel, click the **Swatches** tab.

Press **Ctrl-D** to make sure that nothing is selected.

Eyedropper Tool Icon

Add the first colour to the **Colors** panel by clicking the **Eyedropper** tool on a colour in the logo and then moving the mouse pointer into the grey area under the swatches. It turns into a **Paint Bucket** tool, so just click again.

Add all your logo colours!

Click the **Options** box at the top right of the **Colors** panel. Select **Save Swatches**, and save your swatch as **LogoSwatch** in your **Components** folder.

Options Icon

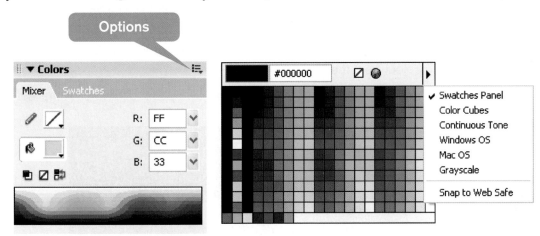

Figure 11.5: Swatches panel

Adding text and a dotted line

Return to your **RockJump** postcard.

Make a new layer and call it **TextLayer**.

Using the **Text** tool, type **Rock Jump**. Use the **Colors** panel to pick the light blue colour from the logo.

Click **Modify**, **Transform**, **Distort**. Try to match the text to Figure 11.6. I am trying to make the text look as though it is lying on the water.

Figure 11.6: Text on water

Tip:

By doing lots of sketching, you will develop a good understanding of how perspective works – extremely useful in the world of graphics. Remember that as objects get further away, they appear smaller. Try to look at the direction shadows are cast and how reflections work on different surfaces.

Pen Icon

⦿ Click the **Pen** tool and set the **Tip size** to **10**, the **Stroke category** to **Dashed**, **Heavy Dash**. Use a colour from the logo.

⦿ Draw an arc from the launch point to the splash-down point; double-click the last point to finish the line.

Figure 11.7: Jump line

⦿ You can add an arrowhead to the line by going to **Commands**, **Creative**, **Add Arrowheads**.

Tip:

The line and the arrowhead will be grouped together, so use the **Subselection** tool if you decide to change their colours.

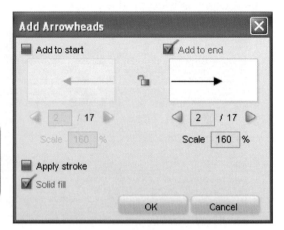

Figure 11.8: Adding arrowheads

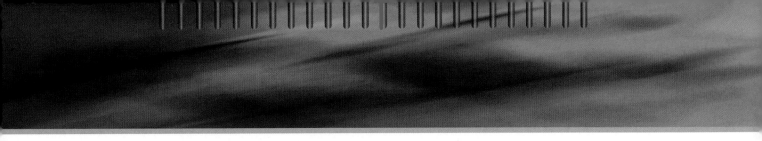

 Add three more text objects: **Jump**, **Free Fall** and **Impact Zone**. Use a colour from the **LogoSwatch** and make sure they are three separate pieces of text, as we will need to move them independently.

Figure 11.9: Journey to the Impact Zone

 Copy and paste the logo into the top left corner of your postcard.

 Play with the **Layer Blend modes** and colours. I added a splash made with the **Pen** tool – my effort is in Figure 11.10.

Figure 11.10: Rock jumper

 Save your card as **RockJumpV2** in the **D203Exercises** folder.

Masks can be created to cover existing objects and determine the area of the image that is visible. We'll start by doing a practice exercise to understand exactly how they work.

- Create a new canvas with a **Width** of **1200 Pixels**, a **Height** of **850 Pixels**, a **Resolution** of **72 Pixels/Inch**, and the **Canvas color** set to **Transparent**.

- Press **Ctrl-0** (**Ctrl** and **zero**), the shortcut to **Fit All**. (Alternatively, use the **Zoom** tool, right-click on the canvas and select **Fit All**.)

- Go to **File**, **Import (Ctrl-R)**. Choose **Archery.jpg** from **DownloadedImages**, and click **Open**.

- Drag the right-angle icon to fit easily in the canvas and then release it.

Figure 12.1   © Acorn Adventure

The first mask we will create will be a vector ellipse.

Ellipse Icon

- Use the vector **Ellipse** tool to draw an ellipse over the centre of the picture. You can use any **Fill** colour, and you don't need a Stroke (see Figure 12.2).

Figure 12.2: Creating a mask object

With the mask selected, choose **Edit**, **Cut** from the **Menu** bar.

Select the original image and, from the **Menu** bar, choose **Edit**, **Paste as Mask**.

Only the part of the image that is inside the mask is now visible.

Figure 12.3

Look in the **Layers** panel. The bitmap object shows both the image and the mask. The two objects are linked, shown by a little chain between them.

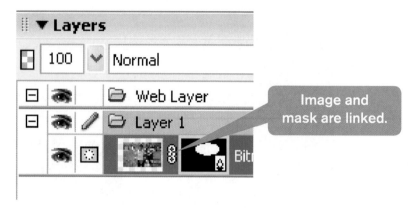

Figure 12.4

Pointer Icon

Try moving the masked image using the **Pointer** tool. The image and mask move together. You can, however, unlink the image from the mask and move it separately.

Click the link between the image and mask in the **Layers** panel so that it disappears.

Now try moving the mask. You can mask a different part of the picture.

Figure 12.5: Moving the mask separately from the image

Notice that the mask, not the image, is currently selected in the **Layers** panel. You can select the image and move or size it.

Click between the image and the mask to relink the two objects. Now you can move them together.

When you have finished experimenting, drag the object (image and mask) onto the trashcan to delete it.

A bitmap mask

Now we will try a bitmap mask, which we will create using the **Brush** tool. This is the technique we will use for the montage.

 Import the **Archery.jpg** file again, and make it a similar size to what it was before.

 Select the **Bitmap** object by clicking its thumbnail in the **Layers** panel, and click the **Add Mask** icon.

In the **Layers** panel, a **Mask** symbol appears in the object box.

Add Mask Icon

 Click the **Brush** tool in the **Tools** panel. Choose a brush size of **80** with **Basic**, **Soft Rounded** stroke category and **100%** opacity.

Brush Icon

You can use a useful shortcut to make your masking easier.

 Make sure you are working on a mask layer, and in your **Tools** panel find the **Colors** section. Make the **Stroke color** box **white** and the **Fill color** box **black**.

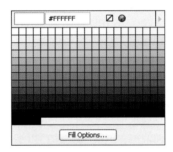

Figure 12.6: Setting the mask colour

 Press **X** on the keyboard and you will notice they swap position.

 Paint with your mask and press **X** to reverse what you have done.

Figure 12.7: A softer mask

Delete this layer without saving. We're ready for the real thing!

Making a montage

In this exercise we will make a montage of images – it will be up to you where you place them but I will add lots of explanations as we go.

We will use layer masks to make the images merge together. You will need to use your artistic skills to blend each image, using natural boundaries such as an arm or a rock to make breaks or borders between images. Get good at this and you will be on your way to a career in the graphics world.

Using secondary sources

For the montage, we will use nine photographs originally downloaded from the website **www.acornadventure.co.uk** and saved on the Payne-Gallway website. Remember to enter all secondary images in your **Elements** table, acknowledge the sources and get permission to use them if necessary. (Permission has already been kindly given by the managing director of Acorn Adventure to use these photographs for this purpose.)

To show what the original photographs looked like, you could take a screenshot of the thumbnail view of your **DownloadedImages** folder for inclusion in your eportfolio.

Figure 12.8: Thumbnails of the downloaded images

Importing images for the montage

▶ Create a new canvas with a **Width** of **1200 Pixels**, a **Height** of **850 Pixels**, a **Resolution** of **72 Pixels/Inch**, and the **Canvas color** set to **Transparent**.

▶ Press **Ctrl-0** (**Ctrl** and **zero**), the shortcut to **Fit All**. (Alternatively, use the **Zoom** tool, right-click on the canvas and select **Fit All**.)

▶ Go to **File, Import (Ctrl-R)**. Choose **RaftBuilding.jpg** from **DownloadedImages**, and click **Open**.

▶ Drag the right-angle icon to the approximate size you want and release. Position and size the image to match Figure 12.9. To resize without distorting an image, hold down the **Shift** key while you drag a corner handle.

Figure 12.9: Importing an image

▶ Import all the pictures in the order below, sizing and positioning them roughly as in Figure 12.10. You need to make sure all the images are overlapping each other by quite a bit, so that you can blend one image into the other without the transparent background showing through.

1. (**RaftBuilding.jpg** – done already)
2. **Climbing.jpg**
3. **WigglyWorm.jpg**
4. **GorgeScrambling.jpg**
5. **Archery.jpg**
6. **Squeezes.jpg**
7. **ArdecheRapid.jpg**
8. **Rafting.jpg**
9. **DeterminedKayaking.jpg**

▶ Rename the layer objects (currently all called **Bitmap**) using these file names.

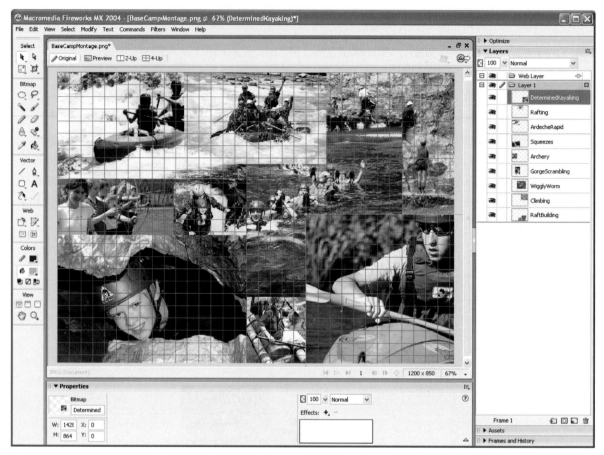

Figure 12.10: Montage before blending

Blending the images using masks

Add Mask Icon

Let's start with **Squeezes**. Select the **Squeezes** layer by clicking its name in the **Layers** panel, then click the **Add Mask** icon.

In the **Layers** panel, a **Mask** symbol appears in the **Squeezes** object box.

Figure 12.11

Remember that you can select either the mask or the image in the object box. If you want to move or paint the image, select the image. If you want to move or paint the mask, select the mask.

Click the **Brush** tool in the **Tools** panel. Choose a large **Basic**, **Soft Rounded** brush with about **50%** opacity. (Using a 50% opacity will allow you to blend the different images more easily.)

Use the shortcut (explained again below) to make creating your montage easier and faster.

▶ Make sure you are working on a mask object, and in your **Tools** panel make the **Stroke color** box **black** and the **Fill color** box **white**.

▶ Paint with your **Brush** tool and press **X** if you want to reverse what you have done. You can use this procedure on all your masks so remember to set the **Stroke** and **Fill** colours as the first thing you do each time.

▶ Paint out the rocks to show the archer, as shown in Figure 12.12.

Paint out the rocks to show the archer.

Figure 12.12: Blending the images

▶ Click on the **Archery** layer, then click the **Add Mask** icon.

▶ From the **Tools** panel, choose the **Paintbrush** tool, **Stroke** colour **black** and **Fill** colour **white**. Merge the **Archery** layer into the **Gorge Scramble**.

▶ Continue in a clockwise direction, adding masks and carefully blending the images into each other.

Tip:

Use the **Pointer** tool to find out which image may need to be masked. You can also move or resize the images if you need to.

Use the Pointer tool to find out which image may need to be masked. You can also move or resize the images if you need to.

Figure 12.13: Take care!

Tip:

Don't forget that you can use **Ctrl** and **Space bar** to zoom in. Press the **Alt** button as well to zoom out, and keep the **Space bar** pressed while you scroll around the canvas!

Here is my montage.

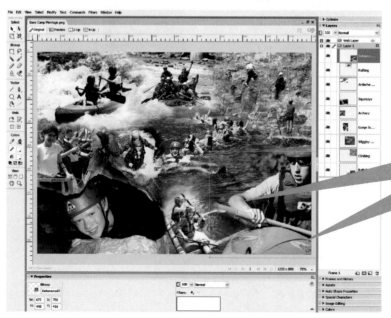

Note that I didn't have to make a mask on every layer.

I used the Lasso tool to make a selection on the arm, which I didn't want to be faded. I also added two Base Camp logos to the canoe.

Figure 12.14: Montage

 Save your montage as **BaseCampMontage.png** in the **D203Exercises** folder.

Chapter 13 - Cut-outs

In this chapter you will learn how to make neat **cut-outs**. This generally involves taking a photo of a product and very neatly cutting it out and placing it on a different background.

Tracing round the image

We will cut out a picture of someone jumping on an aerial tramway and give her a new background to make a much more punchy image. We will use this image later in the Base Camp web page.

Figure 13.1: Jump   © *Acorn Adventure*

- Open picture **RopesHighLeap.jpg** from your **DownloadedImages** folder.

- Click the **Pen** tool; we are going to draw a vector path around the jumping figure.

- Make sure the **Properties inspector** shows the **Fill** set to **None** and the **Stroke** set to **1 pixel** and **Pencil, 1-Pixel Hard** – see Figure 13.2.

Figure 13.2: Pen tool properties

Before starting to draw the path, you need to zoom in so that you can see individual pixels. This will help you to get the most accurate path around the jumper.

- By pressing **Ctrl** and the **Space bar** you can click to **zoom in** whilst the **Pen** tool is selected. (If you add the **Alt** key as well you will **zoom out**.)

- Pressing the **Space bar** on its own gives you the **Hand** tool, which you can use to click and drag the canvas in any direction.

⊙ Draw a path all the way round the jumper as accurately as possible.

Tip:

Use the **Subselection** tool to tweak the path. Add extra nodes to your path by clicking the **Pen** tool on the path. Drawing the path is the most accurate way of cutting out; you could use the **Lasso** tool but it is very difficult to get good results.

Figure 13.3: Carefully draw around the edge

Figure 13.4: The completed path

Creating the bitmap mask

⊙ With the path selected, change its **Fill** colour to match its **Stroke** colour.

⊙ From the **Menu** bar, select **Modify**, **Flatten Selection** to convert the vector path to a bitmap image. We will then be able to make a bitmap mask which we can edit with the **Brush** tool.

⊙ From the **Menu** bar, select **Edit**, **Cut**.

⊙ Select the background bitmap image.

⊙ From the **Menu** bar, select **Edit**, **Paste as Mask**.

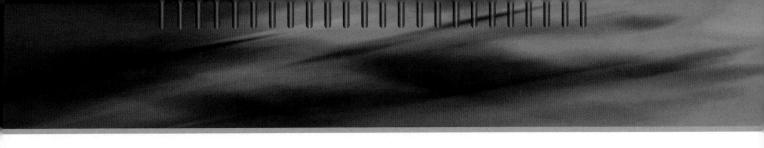

Your image should look like Figure 13.5. Save it as **HighLeap.png** in your **D203Exercises** folder.

Figure 13.5: Cut-out

Taking your own photos

It looks good, but we now need a background. You can find one in several ways; one of the best ways is to go outside with a digital camera and shoot a piece of sky. Each digital camera has its own way of working, so you'll have to read the instructions that come with your particular camera.

Which resolution setting?

Some cameras have a choice of image resolutions. Images that you take with a digital camera for printing out on photographic paper are best taken at the highest resolution your camera allows. However, for this project, all the photos will be viewed on-screen in the eportfolio. On-screen images are viewed at a resolution of 72 pixels per inch (or **dpi**, dots per inch). This means that you can get away with using a lower-quality setting. It is always worth using the lowest setting you need; this prevents wasting space in your camera's memory, and also reduces the amount of optimization you need to do on the photo later on (remember that there is a limit on the file size you are allowed for the eportfolio).

- For your project, a 1 Megapixel (or even 640 x 480 VGA) setting will be fine if you don't plan to enlarge a photo.

- If you are taking a photo that you might want to enlarge significantly, you should use a higher resolution setting (3M or 5M).

These photos will still have relatively large file sizes and be of a higher quality than needed for web purposes. You will learn to optimize photos and images later.

Viewing your photos in Windows Explorer

After you have downloaded your photos onto a computer, you will need to view them to select which ones you want to use. The easiest way to do this is to use Windows Explorer.

Views Icon

- Open Windows Explorer and locate your **DownloadedImages** folder.
- At the top of the window, click the **Views** icon in the **Shortcuts** bar. Select **Filmstrip** from the menu that appears. Use this to flick through your photos and decide which ones to use.

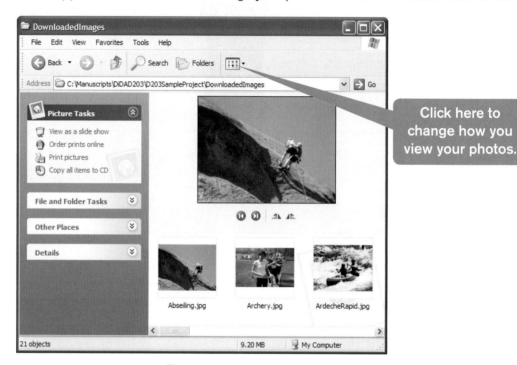

Figure 13.6: Viewing pictures

> **Tip:**
>
> If there is no **Filmstrip** option shown, this may be because you have some movie files in that folder, so move them to another folder. If you still have no **Filmstrip** option, just double-click each photo to see a larger version of it. If you are using a different version of **Windows**, click the **Thumbnails** option.

When you come to download your own photos from the camera to a PC, you should give sensible names to any that you think you will use, so that you can easily find them again later. Delete any that you won't use, so you don't end up with far too many photos!

Finding a ready-made background photo

Sometimes you will have to use an image from a library of photographs. When picking an image, you will need to be very critical about the quality of the photo. There is a lot we can do to fix colours and some damage, but if the photo suffers from a very poor resolution or 'noise' – a common problem of digital photography, caused by too little light – it would be better to carry on looking or to re-shoot it yourself.

Figure 13.7: Backgrounds

There are a number of sites that have free images. Try http://www.freeimages.co.uk/.

Loading a background

We will use one of the images in the **DownloadedImages** folder as a background for the cut-out.

> **!Tip:**
>
> If you want to use your own background image, check that it is only around 1000 pixels wide; we don't need the image any bigger. If your image is too large, go to **Modify**, **Canvas**, **Image Size** and change it to 1000 pixels wide. To see the whole image on the canvas, click the **Zoom** tool, right-click on the canvas and select **Fit All**.

 Load **Clouds.jpg**.

Click the **HighLeap.png** tab at the top of the canvas window.

Select the thumbnail image of the jumper, and press **Ctrl-C** to copy the **Background** layer with its mask attached.

Click back to the **Clouds** image, and press **Ctrl-V** to paste in the jumper.

121

Fixing problems

First, notice that the sun is on the wrong side of the jumper.

▶ To fix this, select the **Jumper** layer and from the **Menu** bar select **Modify**, **Transform**, **Flip Horizontal**.

▶ In the **Properties inspector**, add a **live filter**: Select **Adjust Colour**, **Brightness/ Contrast** and change the settings to make the jumper look a bit punchier.

You may notice that the cut-out is not perfect. You can make adjustments to the mask, as follows:

▶ Click on the mask in the **Layers** panel; a selection box will appear around it, as shown in Figure 13.8.

Figure 13.8: Mask

▶ Choose a small brush and load it with black. The **Properties inspector** should look like the one below.

Figure 13.9: Mask brush options

Remember that if you paint **black**, you will add more masking paint and you will mask the image to show what is behind it. If you paint **white**, you will remove part of the mask.

▶ Try it first. Paint black over the image and notice how you can see through it now. Press **Ctrl-Z** to undo what you have done.

▶ Now go around the edges and carefully clean up any problems. I had to use a 2-pixel brush around the fingers.

> **! Tip:**
> You might prefer to use the **Pencil** tool for this; you can use it to edit the individual pixels.

▶ As a final touch, I used a **live filter** on the cloud background. Select **Adjust Colour**, **Hue/ Saturation**. Check the **Colorize** box and use the sliders to make a nice sky blue.

All done!

Figure 13.10: Free as a bird!

Save your picture as **HighLeapSky.png** in **D203Exercises** and close it.

We are going to use the montage we created in Chapter 12, and some other images we have completed, to produce a brochure front and back cover.

Combining objects into one layer

 Open **BaseCampMontage.png**.

We need to combine all the objects into a single object (called **flattening**), because the result will be much easier to use.

 Select **Layer 1** in the **Layers** panel. This automatically selects all the objects within it.

 Go to **Modify**, **Flatten Selection**. You are left with a single object in the layer.

Because the **.png** format retains information such as the fact that the images bled off the edge of the canvas, you need to change the canvas size.

 Go to **Modify**, **Canvas**, **Canvas Size**. It should read **1200** pixels by **850**. Click **OK**. You will notice the blue selection line jump back to the canvas edges.

 Save the file as **BaseCampMontageFlat.png** in the **D203Exercises** folder.

 Close this file.

Making a brochure cover

In this exercise we will use the montage, with effects added, as a background for a brochure cover.

 Open your saved **BrochureInside.png**, which should be in the **D203Exercises** folder.

 Select and delete the text and resave this file into the same folder, giving it the new file name **BrochureFrontAndBackCover.png**.

 Check that the grid is visible (**View**, **Grid**, **Show Grid**) and the guides are all in position. Go to **View**, **Guides**, **Edit Guides**, and change the guides to a bright red if they aren't already.

Rounded Rectangle Icon

 Draw a vector **Rounded Rectangle** on what will be the front cover (right-hand side).

Ellipse Icon

 Draw an **Ellipse** on the back cover. Copy and paste it three times, using the grid to make the cover look like mine in Figure 14.1.

Tip:

You can easily get the top and bottom ellipses in the right position by snapping them to the grid. You can then select all four ellipses and use **Modify**, **Align**, **Distribute Heights** to set the vertical positions of the middle two ellipses.

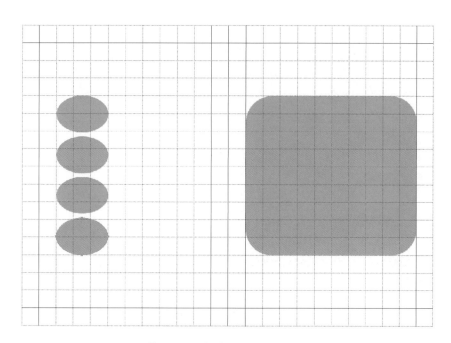

Figure 14.1: Laying out the brochure

We can combine the shapes with a rectangle covering the whole canvas so that the green shapes will become holes through which images will be visible.

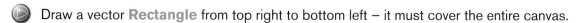 Draw a vector **Rectangle** from top right to bottom left – it must cover the entire canvas.

Rectangle Icon

 Select all the objects by clicking on the layer name, **Layer 1**.

Go to **Modify**, **Combine Paths**, **Join**.

Now change the **Fill** colour in the **Properties inspector** to the dark blue colour from the logo. Remember that you can load your custom colours by clicking **Window**, **Swatches** on the **Menu** bar.

Use a **live filter** (**effect**) **Shadow and Glow** to add a **Drop Shadow**, which must go from left to right.

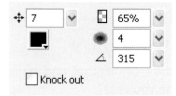

Figure 14.2: Drop Shadow options

Drag the **Composite Path** object in the **Layers** panel down to the **New Bitmap Image** icon to duplicate the layer.

New Bitmap Image Icon

Call the original composite path **Shape1** and the duplicated one above it **Shape2**.

125

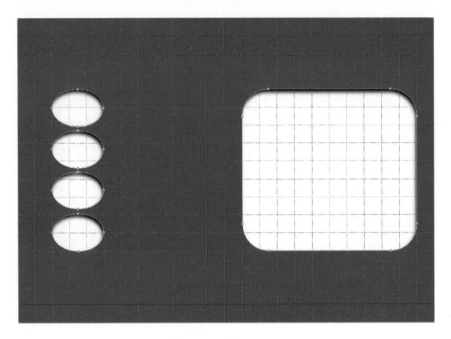

Figure 14.3: Next stage

Adding an image as a vector mask

This bit is really cool!

- Select **File**, **Import** and choose the **BaseCampMontageFlat.png**.
- Draw the imported bitmap right across the canvas.
- Go to **Edit**, **Cut**.
- Select the layer **Shape2** and go to **Edit**, **Paste Inside**.

I want to experiment with using this image in a more arty way by changing the canvas colour to a colour from the logo.

- Select **Modify**, **Canvas**, **Canvas Color** and click the **Custom Color** box.
- Select the dark blue from the logo and click **OK**.
- Select the **Shape2** layer with the **Pointer** tool, and in the **Layers** panel change the **Blend modes** until you find one you like.

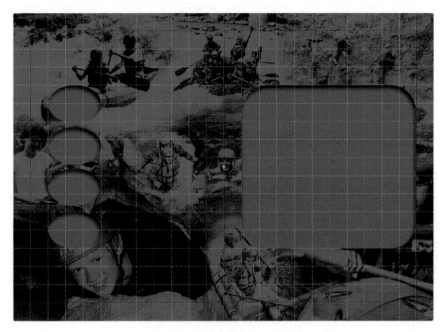

Figure 14.4

Adding pre-prepared graphics

▶ Open the Base Camp logo, **BaseCampLogo.png**.

▶ Select all its objects and go to **Modify**, **Group**. This will group all the elements of the logo together so it will be much easier to move.

▶ Click **Edit**, **Copy** and click back to **BrochureFrontAndBackCover.png**.

▶ Make a new layer and click **Edit**, **Paste**. You may get a message asking if you want to resample the image. Click **Don't resample**.

▶ Use the **Scale** tool to position the logo into the right-hand page recess.

▶ Drag the layer containing the logo down so that it is the last layer in the **Layers** panel.

Scale tool Icon

For the following steps you will need the files **CatamaranSailing.png** and **Abseiling.png** from your **DownloadedImages** folder, and **HighLeapSky.png** and **WoodSign.png** from your **D203Exercises** folder.

▶ Open them, and if they are layered bitmap **.png** files, flatten them.

▶ Copy and paste them into **BrochureFrontAndBackCover.png**.

▶ Use the **Scale** tool to make them small enough to fit into the small ellipses when they are positioned. Use **Add mask** to crop them if they need it.

▶ Create a new top layer and add some suitable text.

If you want to, you could make the sun in the logo three-dimensional by selecting it with the **Subselection** tool and choosing a bevel from the **live filters** (**effects**) in the **Properties inspector**.

I even found room for the Base Camp Bunny! He's becoming a familiar face and an old friend, and that's just what we are trying to achieve to strengthen the brand.

 Save the cover in your **D203Exercises** folder.

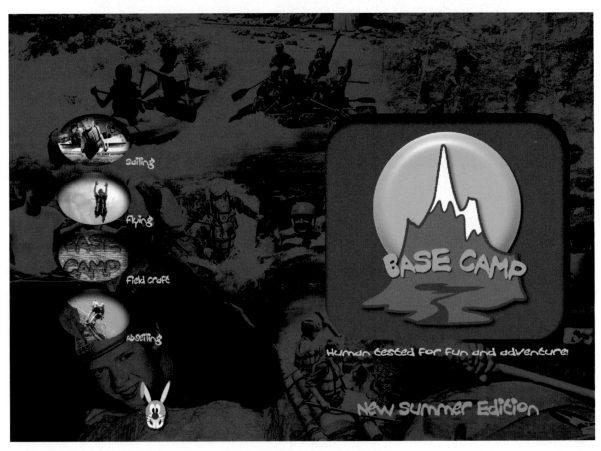

Figure 14.5: Finished brochure cover

 Close all of your files.

Chapter 15 – Fixing Problems with Photos

This chapter will cover some elements you have already learned, but I hope you will see that it is much more in the context of how you could use Fireworks at home, college or the office. With that in mind, you could use digital photos or pictures you may have scanned to complete these projects. Alternatively, you can use photos downloaded from the Payne-Gallway website.

As well as fixing problems with photos, we'll look at capturing screenshots and improving scanned images.

Removing red-eye

First of all, we are going to look at ways of touching up a photograph that you might, for example, want to post on a website or e-mail to a friend.

Red-eye is a common problem in photography, happening when the camera flash reflects from the eye. We can use Fireworks to remove this unsightly effect.

You either need a picture of a friend with a bad case of red-eye, or you can download the image **Bill.jpg** from **www.payne-gallway.co.uk**.

Figure 15.1: Photo of Bill with red-eye

🔘 Open your photo in Fireworks.

If you are using **Bill.jpg**, you first need to rotate the image.

🔘 From the **Menu** bar, select **Modify**, **Canvas**, **Rotate 90 CW**.

> **Tip:**
>
> If you use **Modify, Transform, Rotate 90 CW**, it will rotate the layer but not the canvas, leaving you with a canvas that does not match the image size.

*Oval Marquee
Icon*

Zoom in on one of Bill's eyes so that you can get the most accurate possible selection.

Select the **Oval Marquee** tool and, in the **Properties inspector**, set the **Style** to **Normal** and the **Edge** to **Feather**, **2**. We want to soften the selected edge to make our changes undetectable.

Draw a selection over Bill's eye, covering the whole of the coloured iris.

With the **Shift** key held down, draw another selection over the other eye. You can press **Ctrl-Z** to undo it if you don't place it perfectly the first time.

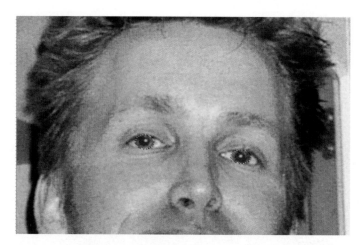

Figure 15.2: Selecting the red eyes

In the **Menu** bar, go to **Filters**, **Adjust Color**, **Hue/Saturation**. Adjust the settings, you will need to reduce the **Saturation** and move the **Hue** to your chosen eye colour. Don't change the **Lightness**, as it will muddy the image. Click **OK** when you're done.

This time go to **Filters**, **Adjust Colour**, **Brightness/Contrast**. By tweaking the contrast you can eliminate unwanted reflections or highlights. Have a play and find the most realistic-looking setting.

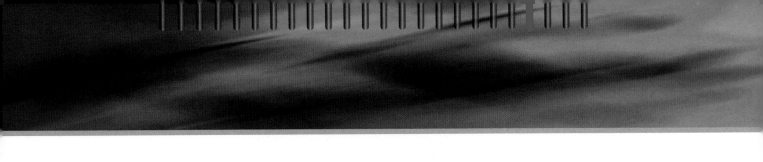

Figure 15.3: Fixed

▶ For some fun, we will add a picture frame. From the **Menu** bar, select **Commands**, **Creative**, **Add Picture Frame**.

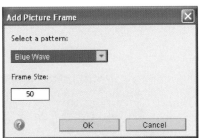

Figure 15.4: Add Picture Frame

▶ Choose a **pattern** and type in a **Frame Size** and press **OK**. You can undo and choose different options to explore what Fireworks has to offer.

Note:

The frame is automatically added as a new object, so you have the option to switch it on and off.

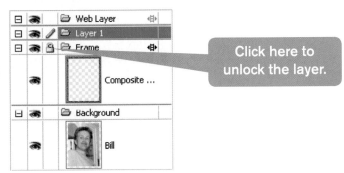

Figure 15.5: Padlock

▶ Add a drop shadow to the frame. You will need to go to the **Layers** panel and click the **Padlock** to unlock the layer.

131

Figure 15.6: All done

 Save the image as **FixedRedEye.png** in your **D203Exercises** folder.

Scratched and dusty old photos

You will need a scan with a bad case of old age, or you can download this image from **www.payne-gallway.co.uk**.

Figure 15.7: Old photo in need of fixing

 Open the picture called **Stuart.jpg**.

 The image is quite faded, so go to **Filters**, **Adjust Color**, **Auto Levels**.

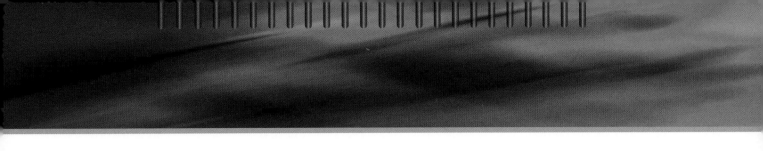

▶ On really bad photos like this one, you will need to use the **Rubber Stamp** tool to fix the cracks and creases. See how good you can make it.

▶ Lastly, choose the **Marquee** tool to draw a square just inside the white frame of the photo. Go to **Select**, **Select Inverse** and paint the selection white. That will help clean up the photo.

*Marquee tool
Icon*

Figure 15.8: Finished job

▶ Produce a **Before and After** image to show how good your re-touching skills are!

▶ Save the final result in your **D203Exercises** folder and close the file.

Sharpening blurred images

Quite often, images are blurred. There is a filter that can help solve this problem. However, although images that are blurred can be made usable, they will never be as good as a sharp original!

We will load a blurred image and experiment with some **Sharpening** effects.

▶ Open **GamblingLights.jpg**.

Figure 15.9: Blurred image

There are two preset sharpening filters: **Sharpen** and **Sharpen More**. These are designed to tighten up most images.

🔘 Go to **Filters**, **Sharpen**, **Sharpen**.

🔘 Now undo and redo (using **Ctrl-Z** and **Ctrl-Y**) to observe how much the **Sharpen** filter affected the image.

🔘 Undo the **Sharpen** effect and try the **Sharpen More** filter. Undo it again.

🔘 Now try the **Unsharp Mask**; this does actually sharpen the image despite its name. I always use the **Unsharp Mask** as it gives me more control.

Figure 15.10: Unsharp Mask panel

🔘 Produce **Before** and **After** images to show how well it works.

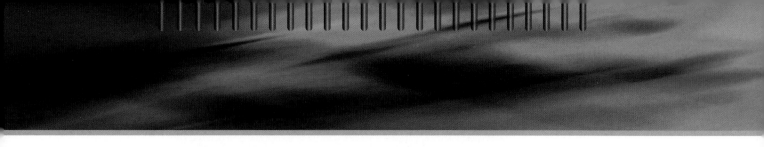

Figure 15.11: Fixed

Note that if you sharpen the image too much you will get white haloing effect and the image will break up into blocks of colour.

Figure 15.12: The haloing effect

Print Screen

This is a very useful function to capture an image of what is on your screen. You might use it if you are surfing the web and you find some information you need, or if you need a screen grab to show how you created a particular graphic. You can try it out now.

It doesn't matter if you have Fireworks running or not.

Press the **Print Screen** key at the top of your keyboard. This will copy a snapshot of your screen to the **Clipboard**.

Open Fireworks if it is not already open.

Select **File**, **New**.

The **Canvas Size** and **Image Size** will be set already, depending on the size and resolution of your screen.

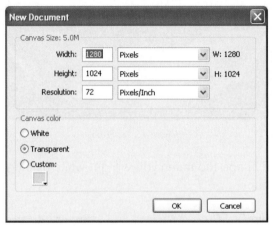

Figure 15.13

Click **OK**.

Click **Edit**, **Paste** (**Ctrl-V**), and the screen grab will appear. You can crop or change it like any raster image.

An alternative to using **Print Screen** is to use a screen capture utility program – there are many free ones available that are good.

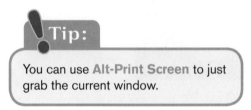

Tip:

You can use **Alt-Print Screen** to just grab the current window.

Fixing problems with scanned images

We covered the basics of scanning in Chapter 7. When you scan a page, remember that you could be infringing copyright if you use it without permission.

Before you start scanning, work out how large you want the image to be in the web page or printed page you are going to produce. Then make sure you use a suitable resolution for either screen or print.

Sometimes you may get a **moiré** effect, as in Figure 15.14, which makes the scan appear patterned or stripey. Here are a few ideas to get around this problem. Trying to fix images is not an exact science – in most cases you can only improve an image; getting a perfect result is rare.

Figure 15.14: Moiré effect

You can see the moiré pattern appear, and it will look much worse in print than it looks on screen. You can get rid of it, or at least make it better, by scanning the image at full resolution.

- You could try scanning the cover of this book or a magazine!

- When your image is scanned into Fireworks, go to **Filters**, **Noise**, **Add noise**. This will help break up the moiré print screen; you will need less than **10** as the **Amount**.

- Then use **Modify**, **Canvas**, **Image size** to resize your scan depending on how you plan to use it. It will pay to repeat the process with varying amounts of noise. Even slightly changing the scan resolution may help.

The Base Camp dollar

In this chapter we will look at producing artwork for print. The Base Camp dollar note will be used instead of money within the camp, so it obviously has to be printed. Artwork for high-quality printed material (such as this book) requires a resolution of **300dpi** to ensure that images are smooth and not pixellated.

Images using such a high resolution will result in files much larger than anything we have produced so far. A large layered computer file can run into many hundreds of megabytes! Because all your artwork has to be shown in an eportfolio, we will use a resolution of **72dpi** for the design of the dollar note. For this exercise, we only need to show one side.

It will help your design if you find some images of paper money… you might even have some in your wallet. Measure different notes and decide on a good size for the new dollar note. Have a look at what is printed on the front and back of a note, and what sort of background is used. Make a list of elements you need to include.

 Create a new canvas with a **Width** of **14 cm**, a **Height** of **7.5 cm**, a **Resolution** of **72 Pixels/Inch**, and the **Canvas color** set to **White**.

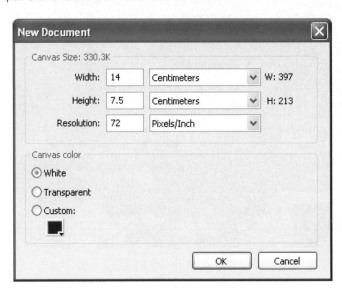

Figure 16.1: Settings for the Base Camp dollar

Creating the background

First of all, we will create the intricate background found on money as a deterrent to forgery.

 Press **Ctrl-0** to fit your canvas onto the screen.

 Choose the **Pen** tool and change the **Stroke** to **black**, the **Size** to **2**, the **Stroke category** to **Pencil**, **1-Pixel Hard** and the **Edge** to **0** so you get a hard-edged line.

Pen Tool Icon

Draw a single wavy line across the canvas, starting and ending the line slightly off your canvas, as shown in Figure 16.2.

Figure 16.2: Wavy line

Click the **Pointer** tool and select the line. As you start to move it down press the **Shift** key and the **Alt** key, which will drag-copy the line and keep it in the same vertical plane.

Pointer Icon

Go to **Edit**, **Repeat Duplicate** (**Ctrl-Y**) and keep duplicating until you cover the canvas. Keep going into the grey at the bottom of the canvas – you will move the wavy lines up in the next step, and need them to completely cover the canvas when you do.

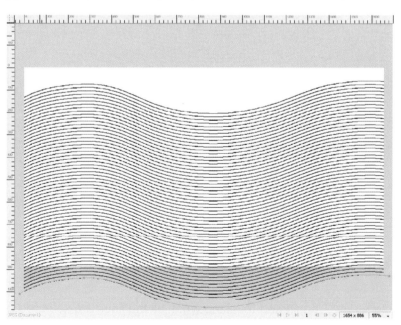

Figure 16.3

Click **Layer 1** in the **Layers** panel to select all your lines, and use the **Pointer** tool to drag all the lines up to cover the canvas.

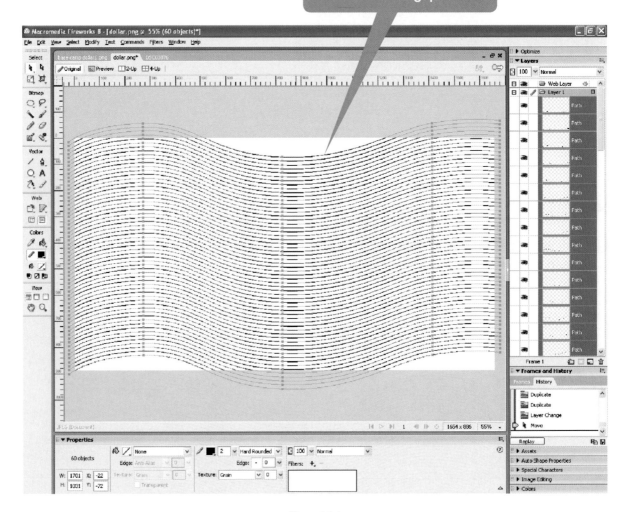

Figure 16.4

We don't need to tweak these vector lines and they are already print size, so we can turn these into a bitmap layer for the next stage.

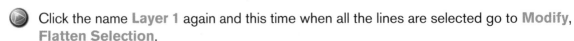 Click the name **Layer 1** again and this time when all the lines are selected go to **Modify**, **Flatten Selection**.

New Bitmap Image Icon

Change the name of this bitmap object from **Bitmap** to **Lines**, and drag it down onto the **New Bitmap Image** icon to make a duplicate of it.

Flip this image using **Modify**, **Transform**, **Flip Horizontal**.

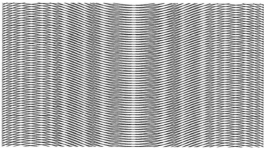

Figure 16.5: Criss-crossed wavy lines

▶ Rename this layer **CrissCrossLines**.

▶ Make a **New Layer** called **GradientBackground** and drag it under **CrissCrossLines**.

▶ Drag the vector **Rectangle** tool right over the canvas: turn off the **Stroke**, choose a **Fill** colour to look like the washy sort of colours used for paper money and add a **Fill Texture**. I chose **Hatch 3** at **50%**.

Rectangle Icon

Figure 16.6: Fill properties for the background

▶ Draw another vector rectangle over the canvas, and this time in the **Properties inspector** select a **Fill category** of **Gradient**, **Bars**.

▶ Click in the **Fill Color** box and choose **Cobalt Blue** from the **Preset**.

▶ At the top of the **Layers** panel, set the **Layer Blend mode** to **Fuzzy Light**. (If you have not got this layer blend, set the **Opacity** to **40%** instead.)

▶ Go back to your **CrissCrossLines** layer, and set the **Opacity** to **30**.

▶ Use the **Crop** tool to trim your wavy lines to the canvas size.

Crop Icon

Figure 16.7: The completed background

▶ Save the image as **BaseCampDollar.png** in the **Dollar** folder.

Adding a photograph and mask

We will add a picture for the note; you can use a picture that you have taken yourself, or use the one I used.

⏵ Open the picture **TorOnDartmoor.jpg**. You should have already downloaded this from **www.payne-gallway.co.uk** into your **DownloadedImages** folder.

⏵ Select it and copy it using either **Edit**, **Copy** or **Ctrl-C**.

⏵ Click back onto the tab for **BaseCampDollar.png**.

⏵ Make a new layer called **Photograph** and paste the picture onto it. You might get a panel asking if you want to resample the image – if so, select **Don't Resample**.

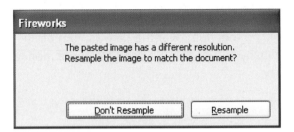

Figure 16.8: Resample or not?

Scale Icon

Add Mask Icon

⏵ Use the **Scale** tool to size and position the image. Draw an **Oval Marquee** tool over the most interesting bit of the picture.

⏵ Press the **Add Mask** icon.

Figure 16.9: Picture cut-out

We will use the **Find edges** filter to make the photo look a bit like an engraving, just like real paper money.

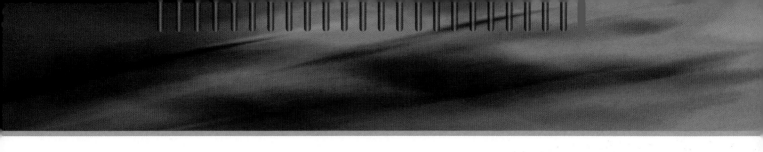

▶ Duplicate the oval photo by dragging the **Bitmap** object onto the **New Bitmap** icon.

▶ In the **Menu** bar, select **Filters, Other, Find Edges.**

▶ The image will be mostly black; let's reverse it so the black becomes white. Go to **Filters, Adjust Colour, Invert.**

▶ Check the order of the layers in the **Layers** panel; you should have **GradientBackground** at the bottom, then **CrissCrossLines**, and **Photograph** at the top.

▶ In **Photograph**, select the image we applied the **Find Edges** filter to. Set the **Opacity** to **66** and the **Blend mode** to **Luminosity.** You can do this either in the **Properties inspector** (if you have the **Pointer** tool selected) or in the **Layers** panel.

▶ Set the unfiltered photo image (underneath the other one in the **Photograph** layer) to **100% Opacity** and set its **Blend mode** to **Screen.**

▶ Draw a vector **Ellipse** around the photo image, drag it under your photo images and set its **Blend mode** to **Luminosity.**

▶ Use the **Scale** tool to tweak it around your photo image so that it looks something like Figure 16.10.

New Bitmap Icon

Scale Icon

Figure 16.10: Adding an ellipse

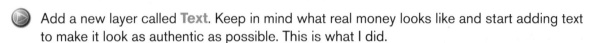

Adding text

It doesn't look much like real money at the moment, so let's add some text. This will be largely up to you – I used frilly **Edwardian** text to give it an authentic look.

🔘 Add a new layer called **Text**. Keep in mind what real money looks like and start adding text to make it look as authentic as possible. This is what I did.

Figure 16.11: Loot!

🔘 Add a serial number! Use the **Scale** tool to spin the text around.

Using the Assets panel

There is one more thing you can do to add realism to your currency.

🔘 Make a new layer called **VectorSymbol**, and make sure it is at the top.

🔘 Open the **Assets** panel in your **Panel** dock. If you can't find it, go to **Window**, **Auto Shapes**.

🔘 In the **Assets** panel there are some extra useful shapes. Click on **Perspective** and drag it onto your canvas. The perspective lines add a little extra interest.

🔘 In the **Layers** panel, change the **Layer Blend mode** to **Overlay** or **Screen**.

🔘 Tweak the layers and see if you can make your Base Camp dollar even better!

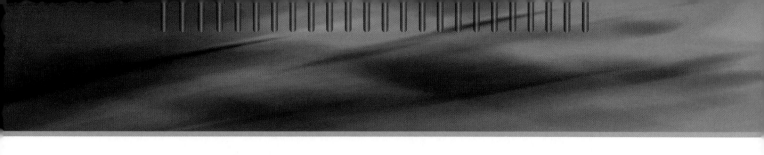

Figure 16.12: The completed Base Camp dollar

 Save your **BaseCampDollar.png** file in the **Dollar** folder.

 Don't forget to make entries for the dollar and the photograph you used, in your **Elements** table in Word.

All our images, by default, use the colour system **RGB**. For printed artwork, this would need to be converted to **CMYK**. You cannot do this in Fireworks, which is a web-based graphics program. The different modes are explained below.

Image modes

Macromedia Fireworks uses a system by which it only deals with screen colours RGB. Fireworks has five different colour modes for you to choose and pick colours from. Some of these colour modes have been outdated simply because modern screens can display millions of colours. Here is a brief explanation of the five main colour modes that you may come across in the world of graphics and printing.

RGB mode

This is a default mode for nearly all images created on the computer. **RGB** uses three colours (also called channels) to reproduce over 16 million colours, many more than the human eye can distinguish. The three colours – **Red**, **Green** and **Blue** – are mixed in values of 0–255. If all three colours were set to zero the result would be black, and if they were all set to 255 the result would be white.

In **RGB** mode this image is 283k.

Figure 16.13: A picture in RGB mode

Indexed Colour mode

This mode uses up to 256 colours. If you convert an **RGB** file to an **Indexed** file, the file size will decrease, but the image quality will also be reduced because it has fewer colours. It has to approximate some of the **RGB** colours. **GIF** files use indexed colours.

In **Indexed Color** mode this image is 94k.

Figure 16.14: A picture in Indexed Colour mode

In **Greyscale** mode this image is 94k.

Greyscale mode

Greyscale uses up to 256 shades of grey. You can scan an image in **Greyscale** mode.

Figure 16.15: A picture in Greyscale mode

Bitmap mode

Bitmap mode assigns one of two colours (black or white) to each pixel in an image. This results in very small file sizes, but unless your image is black and white (for example, text) it will be severely degraded if you save it as a **Bitmap**.

In **Bitmap mode** this image is 12k.

Figure 16.16: A picture in Bitmap mode

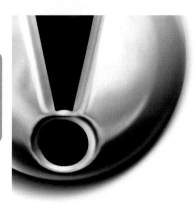

In CMYK mode this image is 377k.

Figure 16.17: A picture in CMYK mode

CMYK mode

CMYK (Cyan, Magenta, Yellow and black) is the printing world standard; Fireworks will not allow you to convert to CMYK! These are the colours of printer's inks and digitally they are mixed from 0 to 100. If you are converting RGB files to CMYK in another piece of software, be aware that bright blues and greens will suffer 'drop off', because the inks cannot print colours as bright as your monitor can display!

Changing Image Modes

Whenever you convert a file to a worse quality mode (for example from RGB to Indexed Colour) you should always save a backup in the original mode. You should also aim to do as much editing as possible in the better colour mode before converting.

Good Marks... ✓

You will get good marks if you:

- show evidence that you have looked at real currency to get ideas for size, patterns, text, and so on
- describe what specifications for resolution and colour you would need for printed material
- produce an authentic-looking note which is fit for purpose and can be identified as the Base Camp currency
- annotate your graphic to show dimensions and special features
- keep a record in the **Elements** table of all of the images you have used or created.

Bad Marks... ✗

You will lose marks if you:

- do not include the essential features of a currency note
- do not annotate your graphic
- save an unnecessarily large graphics file which will take a long time to download.

Chapter 17 – Hotspots, Slices and Rollovers

In this chapter you will be introduced to some of the web-based tools. You can create hotspots, buttons and links in Dreamweaver, but sometimes it is more convenient to create them in Fireworks and, if necessary, edit them later in Dreamweaver.

Hotspots

A hotspot is an area marked out by you, so that when the mouse pointer is moved over that area, an action is performed. Embedded information will take you to another web page or picture. The embedded information that performs the action is called a **hyperlink**.

We will draw a hotspot and link it to a website, which we can preview in a browser.

- Create a new canvas with a **Width** of **800 Pixels**, a **Height** of **600 Pixels**, a **Resolution** of **72 Pixels/Inch**, and set the **Canvas color** to **White**.

- Draw a vector **Rectangle** and **Star** onto the canvas, as shown in Figure 17.1.

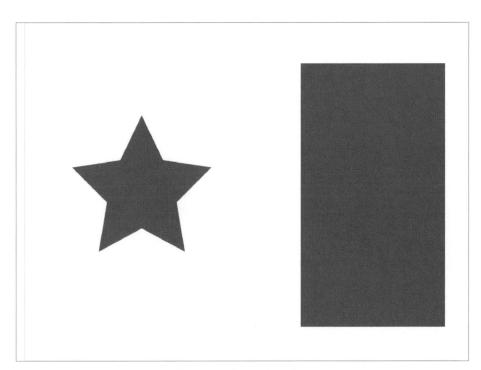

Figure 17.1: Rectangle and star

- In the **Web** section of the **Tools** panel, choose the **Rectangle Hotspot** tool.

- Drag a hotspot over the rectangle shape. You will notice that the hotspot has automatically appeared in the **Web Layer** in the **Layers** panel.

Rectangle Hotspot Icon

We can draw elliptical and custom-shaped hotspots with the **Polygon Hotspot** tool.

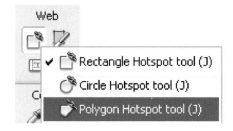

Figure 17.2: Hotspot tools

Subselection Icon

Show/Hide Icon

Pick the **Polygon Hotspot** tool. Click around the star shape.

Use the **Subselection** tool if you need to tweak the shape.

Look in the **Layers** panel. You can show and hide each hotspot by using the **Show/Hide** icon next to the object. You can also hide hotspots with the icon in the **Web** section of the **Tools** panel.

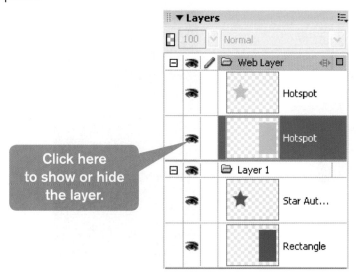

Figure 17.3: Showing and hiding layers

Hotspot Icon

With the **Pointer** tool, click on the **Rectangle Hotspot** and look in the **Properties inspector**.

Creating a hyperlink

First look at the field called **Link**. We will add a **URL** (uniform resource locator) which will tell the browser to perform an action.

Type http://www.google.co.uk. (The **http** stands for **HyperText Transfer Protocol**.) This is the link that will send you to a new web page.

Alt text

The next field is **Alt** field, which specifies the alternative text that will appear while an image is loading or if it cannot be loaded. This text is often displayed by your pointer when you hover over an image on a web page.

 Write **Search engine** into the field.

Target

The **Target** field is the window or frame you want the link to open in. The choices are:

None and **_self**	open the destination page in the same location that the button is in
_blank	opens the destination page in a new browser window
_parent	opens the destination page in the parent frameset of the link
_top	replaces all the frames in the current browser window and opens the destination page in that window.

 Set **Target** to **_blank** so it opens a new browser window.

Figure 17.4: Properties inspector for the rectangle hotspot

 Click the **Star Hotspot** and enter a web address of your own. I entered mine and put a very uncool tag.

Figure 17.5: Properties inspector for the star hotspot

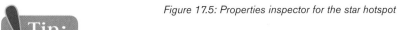

> **Tip:**
>
> There is also a **Color** box, where you can change the colour of the hotspot. This is quite useful if the hotspot is blending into an image!

 You can view your handiwork by going to **File**, **Preview in Browser**, **Preview in iexplore.exe** (**F12** for a shortcut).

The hotspots are invisible now! When you hover your pointer over one of the hotspots, its Alt text appears as a tooltip. Clicking a hotspot opens the target website in a new window.

 Close all of the Internet Explorer windows, save your image as **RectangleAndStar.png** in your **D203Exercises** folder, and close it.

Creating a button

Making buttons in Fireworks is easy, and we can make them change appearance when they are rolled over or pressed. We can add behaviours to display pictures and more. This will give our websites much more interactivity and make them much more fun to use!

Often, if you are looking around a website, you will notice that the buttons and other images or text react as the mouse pointer drifts over them – this is a **rollover** and generally indicates that something will happen if you click the button, image or text.

Although Fireworks has lots of ready-made buttons, it is easier to understand how they work by making one.

 Create a new canvas with a **Width** of **800 Pixels**, a **Height** of **600 Pixels**, a **Resolution** of **72 Pixels/Inch**, and the **Canvas color** set to **White**.

 Go to **Edit**, **Insert**, **New Button**.

The **Button Editor** opens, ready to create a new button. The first four tabs across the top of the editor window enable you to select which state you will create the button in. We will create our button in the **Up** state.

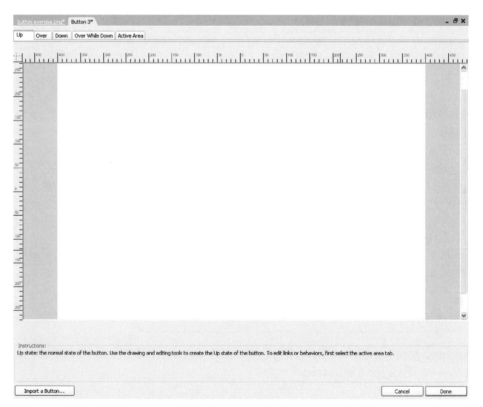

Figure 17.6: Button Editor

 Draw a perfect vector **circle** in the middle of the **Button Editor**, colour it blue, and add a **Bevel** from the **live filters**.

▶ Use the **Text** tool to write **Yes!** on the button.

▶ Use the **Properties inspector** to centre the text in its box.

Figure 17.7

The button should look like Figure 17.8.

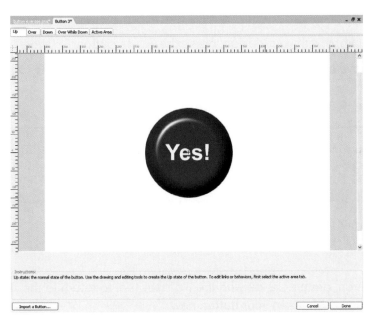

Figure 17.8: Button with bevel and text

If you want the button to look different when it is clicked or when the mouse pointer passes over it, you have to create a button for each state.

▶ At the top of the canvas, click the **Over** tab. This next button will be displayed when the mouse pointer goes over it. Press the **Copy Up Graphic** button at the bottom right of the canvas to start with a copy of the button in its **Up** state.

▶ Select the text and add a **live filter** of type **Shadow and Glow, Glow** to make a nice white glow for the text.

▶ Now press the **Down** tab, to specify what we will see when the button is pressed. Click the **Copy Over Graphic** button. Select the vector button and use the **Edit and arrange live filters** icon to change the bevel so that it looks as though the button has been pressed.

▶ Go to the **Over While Down** and **Copy Over Graphic**. Change the glow to green.

This is what each button should look like. Click the **Up**, **Over**, **Down** and **Over While Down** tabs to compare your buttons with Figure 17.9.

Figure 17.9: All the different states of the new button

 When you are happy with your design, press the **Done** button.

 Press **F12** to have a look at your button in Internet Explorer. Press **F5** to reset the button.

Tip:

You may get the message **To help protect your security, Internet Explorer has restricted this file from showing active content that could access your computer. Click here for options...** You can click and select **Allow blocked content**. Click **Yes** in the pop-up window.

 Close the browser window.

Editing a button

 To edit your button, double-click it with the **Pointer** tool to return to the **Button Editor**. You can make any changes to your button now.

 Click the **Active Area** tab. Fireworks automatically sets a rectangular active area to cover your button. The active area is represented by a **slice** that appears on your screen as a semi-opaque rectangle.

 Select the button (or the active area surrounding it) and look in the **Properties inspector**. You will see you can control it just like a hotspot. We don't need to add a hyperlink now.

 Press **Done**.

 Save the file as **RolloverButton.png** in your **D203Exercises** folder.

Sharing symbols

When you build a website, you will almost certainly need a navigation bar. This will contain several buttons of a similar appearance, which link the user to different pages in the website. You can very quickly create more buttons that look similar to the one that you have just created.

 Open **RolloverButton** if it is not still open.

 Click the **Library** tab in your **Assets** panel in the **Panel** dock. (If the **Assets** panel is not visible, go to **Window**, **Library** in the **Menu** bar.) In there you will see the **Button** symbol.

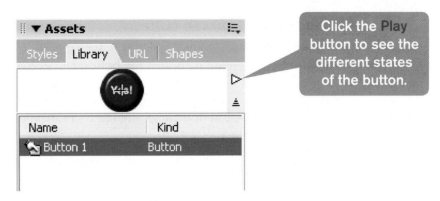

Click the Play button to see the different states of the button.

Figure 17.10: Library

 Click and drag the button into the canvas.

This creates a duplicate button. You can change the text on the button and the link in the **Properties inspector**. Any other changes (such as the bevel or filter) that you make to either button in the **Button Editor** will be applied to both these buttons. Try this as follows.

 In the **Properties inspector**, change the Text to No! then press Enter.

Figure 17.11: Editing the button

The text on the button has changed.

 Double-click the button with the **Pointer** tool to enter the **Button Editor**. (The original button will appear, whichever button you double-click.) Change the **Down State** glow to another colour. Press **Done**.

Figure 17.12

 Press F12 to view your buttons in the browser to see what happens.

Both of the buttons have changed, as they are linked!

This is very useful when you have a set of similar buttons in a navigation bar – if you want to change, say, the colour or size of the buttons, you only need to do this once for each button state.

Creating an unlinked copy of the button

Sometimes you may want a similar button which has, for example, a different colour from those in the navigation bar. You can create a copy of the button and edit it independently of the others, as follows.

New Symbol Icon

In the **Library**, drag the button (the name, not the thumbnail) down onto the **New Symbol** icon.

The **Symbol Properties** dialogue box appears. Set the **Name** to **ColouredButton**, make sure the **Type** is set to **Button** and press **OK**.

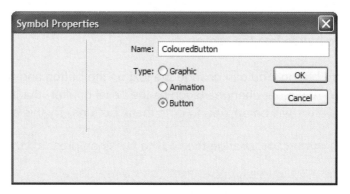

Figure 17.13: Symbol Properties

Drag the new button onto the canvas.

Double-click the button with the **Pointer** tool to enter the **Button Editor**. Change the colour of the button to red in all four button states and press **F12** to view your buttons in a browser again.

Figure 17.14: Two linked buttons and one unlinked button

Save the file as **RolloverButtonV2** in your **D203Exercises** folder.

Close the file.

156

Creating a disjointed rollover

 Create a new canvas with a **Width** of **800 Pixels**, a **Height** of **600 Pixels**, a **Resolution** of **72 Pixels/Inch**, and the **Canvas color** set to **White**.

This time we will create a disjointed rollover, which is a simple way of making images appear when we want them to.

There are four steps involved.

1. Create two frames with different images to display **before** and **after** the rollover is put into action.

2. Mark out with a **slice** object where the image is to be viewed.

3. Add a **hotspot** to trigger the rollover.

4. Assign a **swap image** behaviour to the trigger object.

Let's do it!

Step 1 – Creating two frames with different images

 Click **File**, **Import** (or press **Crtl-R**) to import an image, and find **CatamaranSailing.jpg** from your **DownloadedImages** folder.

 Draw the image out into the canvas, leaving plenty of room around it.

Figure 17.15: Imported catamaran picture

 With the **Text** tool, write **Before** just under the picture.

 Go to **Window**, **Frames** to display the **Frames** panel in the **Panel** dock.

New/Duplicate Frame Icon

Drag **Frame 1** down onto the **New/Duplicate Frame** icon.

Apply a **live filter** of type **Blur, Zoom Blur** to the image (not the text) in **Frame 2**. Change the text to **After**.

Step 2 – Marking out a Slice object

Slice Icon

With the **Slice** tool from the **Web** section of the **Tools** panel, draw a slice over the image and the text. Don't worry too much about accuracy – this is just a practice exercise.

Figure 17.16: Slice

Select **Window, URL** to display the **URL** panel, and set the **Current URL** to **No URL (noHREF)**.

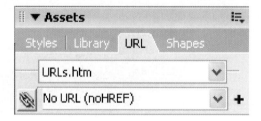

Figure 17.17: URL

Make sure **Frame 1** is selected in the **Frames** panel.

Draw a vector **Arrow** (one of the shapes sharing a button with the vector **Rectangle**) in the white area of the canvas. Use the Scale tool to rotate the arrow so that it points down to the top left corner of the image (as shown in Figure 17.18, but without the blue hotspot rectangle).

Step 3 – Adding a hotspot to trigger the rollover

We can add a hotspot easily. With the vector arrow selected, go to **Edit, Insert, Hotspot**.

Figure 17.18: The rollover so far

Step 4 – Assigning a Swap Image behavior to the trigger object

In the centre of the hotspot is a crosshair icon called the **Behavior controller**. Click on it and drag out from it, and a line will appear.

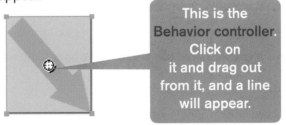

This is the Behavior controller. Click on it and drag out from it, and a line will appear.

Figure 17.19: The Behavior controller

Drag the line onto the **Target slice area** (the catamaran image) and release the mouse.

A **Swap Image** dialogue box will appear – click **OK**.

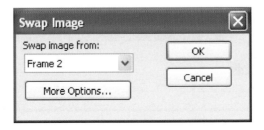

Figure 17.20: Swap Image box

The curved line shows there is a **Swap Image** behaviour between the hotspot and the slice.

Press **F12** to **Preview in Browser** and have a look at what you have done. As your mouse pointer rolls over the arrow, it shows the image on **Frame 2** – simple!

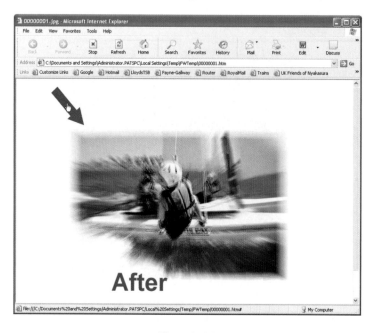

Figure 17.21

Close the browser window.

Behaviors panel

We will have a quick look at the **Behaviors** panel and what it has to offer.

Click on the arrow hotspot.

If the **Behaviors** panel is not visible, click **Window**, **Behaviors** to display it.

Click on **Events** and change it from the default **onMouseOver** to **onClick**. Press **F12** to see how the change has affected your trigger arrow.

Figure 17.22: Behaviors panel

⊙ So that you really understand what is going on, draw another vector **Arrow** on **Layer 1**. (See Figure 17.24.) With the new arrow selected, click **Edit**, **Insert**, **Hotspot**.

⊙ Click on the **Hotspot** and click and drag the **Behavior controller** onto the **Slice** to create a **Swap Image** behaviour between them.

⊙ Set the **Swap Image** window to **Frame 1** and click **OK**.

⊙ Click on the first arrow, click the **Options** button in the top right of the **Behaviors** panel and click **Edit**.

⊙ Uncheck **Restore image onMouseOut**. This will mean that the image will remain on **Frame 2** after the mouse pointer leaves the hotspot. Click **OK**.

⊙ Click on the new arrow hotspot and, in the **Behaviors** panel, make sure **Events** is set to **onClick**.

⊙ Click the **Options** button in the top right of the **Behaviors** panel and click **Edit**.

⊙ Set the **Frame no.** to **Frame 1**. Uncheck **Restore image onMouseOut**. This will cause the image to remain on **Frame 2** once clicked. Click **OK**.

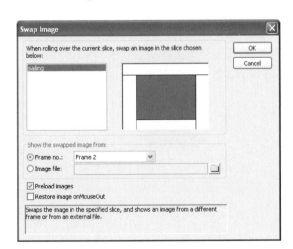 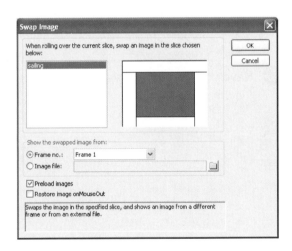

Figure 17.23: Swap Image panels for (a) the first arrow and (b) the second arrow

⊙ Press **F12**, and you will find that you now need to click each arrow to switch between **Before** and **After**.

Figure 17.24

Save your experiment as **DisjointedRollover.png** in the **D203Exercises** file, and close it.

In this chapter we are going to build the web page for Base Camp. We are going to try to make an interactive page that will be interesting and a good advertisement for Base Camp.

We have already created a brochure cover as an exercise, and this cover will make a very good basis for a striking web page. No point letting a perfectly good piece of artwork go to waste!

 Open **BrochureFrontAndBackCover.png**.

 Go to **Modify, Canvas, Image size**. The first step is to re-size the image to **800 pixels** wide. The height will automatically change to **567**. Press **OK**.

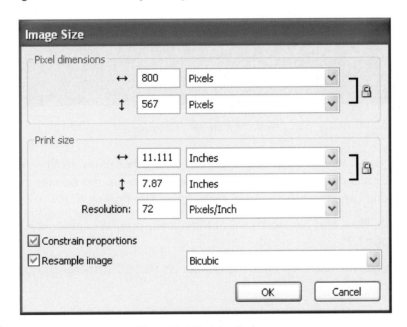

Figure 18.1: Resizing the image

Tip:

A good average web site is 800 x 600.

 Save this as **BaseCampWebPage.png** in the **WebPage** folder.

Creating the text banner

We will make the text **Human tested for fun and adventure** into a banner stretching across the top of the web page.

 Select the text and move it to the top of the page.

 Select **Stretch alignment** in the **Properties inspector** and stretch the banner between the guides by dragging its blue selection handles. Change the font size so that the height is appropriate for the new width.

Stretch alignment Icon

 Add a rounded rectangle and place it under the text.

Bring your **BaseCampBunny** in and place it in your banner; you could add another rounded rectangle to change the shape of your banner (see Figure 18.2).

> **Tip:**
>
> You will need to drag the **BaseCampBunny** to the **Text** layer.

Figure 18.2: Banner on the page

 You can save your banner so you could reuse it on another page. Hold down the **Ctrl** key while you click on each of the four components that make up the banner in the **Layers** pane: the text, the bunny and the two rounded rectangles. Then press **Ctrl-C** to copy.

 Now go to **File**, **New** and Fireworks will automatically open a canvas with the banner size, so you can press **OK**.

 Press **Ctrl-V** to paste, and then save the banner as **BaseCampBanner.png** in your **WebPage** folder.

Figure 18.3: Finished banner on its own

 Close the banner and return to **BaseCampWebPage.png**.

Creating different frames

Be careful when doing this next bit; **Layers** and **Frames** are different!

We are going to create four rollovers, so that when the mouse pointer rolls over one of the thumbnail images on the left, a larger image appears in place of the logo on the right-hand side. The first step is to put each of these images into a different frame. The image with the logo is currently in **Frame 1**.

  In the **Frames and History** panel, drag **Frame 1** on to the **New/Duplicate Frame** icon to create **Frame 2**.

New/Duplicate Frame Icon

● Go to the **Layers** panel and switch off the **Base Camp Logo**.

● Go to **File, Open** to open the first image: **CatamaranSailing.png**.

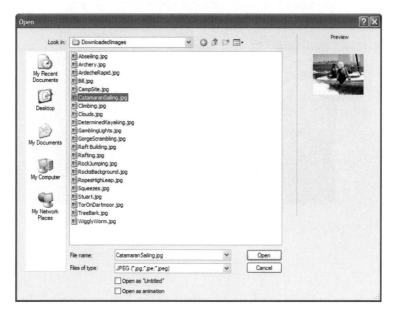

Figure 18.4

● Make sure the image is flattened by going to **Modify, Flatten Layers**. If there is more than one object in the layer, select all the objects and go to **Modify, Flatten Selection**.

● Copy the image.

● Return to **BaseCampWebPage.png**.

● With the layer containing your background images selected, click **Edit, Paste**. If the message shown in Figure 18.5 appears, click **Don't Resample**.

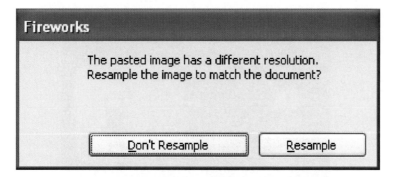

Figure 18.5

● Use the **Scale** tool to position and size the image in the right-hand window in place of the logo.

Scale Icon

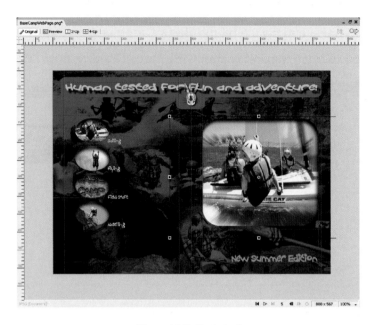

Figure 18.6: Scale tool

New/Duplicate Frame Icon

To see what you have created, click on **Frame 1** in the **Frames** panel. The logo reappears. Click on **Frame 2** and the catamaran appears.

Drag **Frame 2** onto the **New/Duplicate Frame** icon to create **Frame 3**.

Make sure **Frame 3** is selected.

Delete the catamaran picture.

Repeat the steps to put **HighLeapSky.png** from the **D203Exercises** folder into the right-hand window.

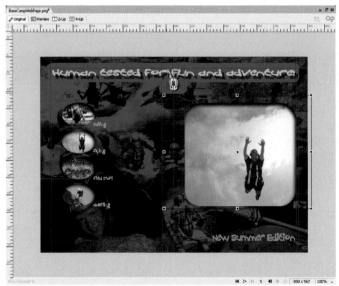

Figure 18.7: Leap!

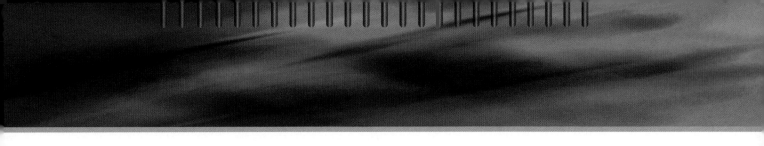

▶ Do the same for the third image, **WoodSign.png**.

▶ You can copy and paste **Abseiling.jpg** in the same way, or read the tip below for a faster method!

Tip:

If your image is an original photograph, it will not have different layers. You can save time by importing the **jpg** image. With your graphics layer selected, click **File**, **Import** to import **Abseiling.jpg**.

Creating the slices

▶ Use the **Slice** tool to draw a slice over the right-hand window (it doesn't matter which frame and layer are selected).

Slice Icon

Figure 18.8: Drawing a slice over the image

Creating hotspots

Next we will create the hotspots for each thumbnail.

▶ In the thumbnail layer, click on the **Sailing** thumbnail.

▶ Go to **Edit**, **Insert**, **Hotspot**.

*Subselection
Icon*

Create hotspots for the other three thumbnails.

Use the **Subselection** tool to move or resize any of the hotspot boxes that are overlapping.

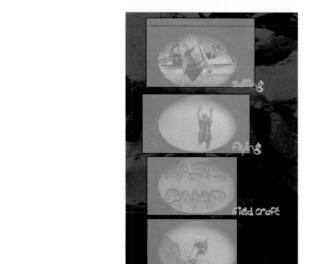

Figure 18.9: Making sure that the hotspots don't overlap

The hotspots have been automatically placed on the web layer.

Re-name the hotspots **Sailing**, **Flying**, **FieldCraft** and **Abseiling**.

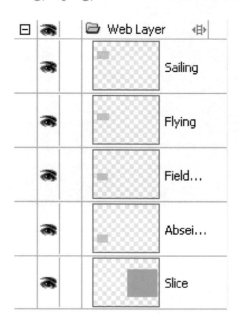

Figure 18.10: Naming the hotspots

Assigning a swap image behaviour

Drag the crosshair from the centre of the first hotspot to the right-hand window (the target slice area). A **Swap Image** dialogue box will appear.

Select **Frame 2** (the catamaran picture) and press **OK**.

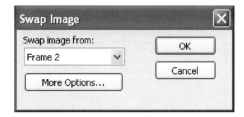

Figure 18.11: Swap Image

Repeat this process for each thumbnail, selecting frames 3, 4 and 5.

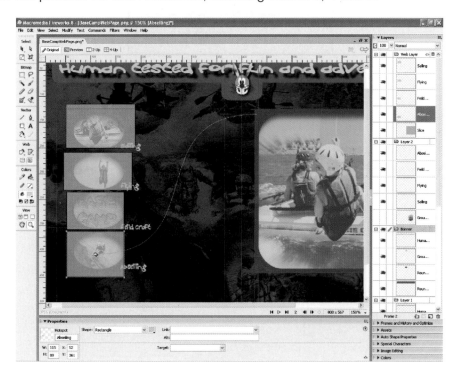

Figure 18.12

Press **F12** to test your rollovers.

When you've taken in the beauty and genius of your creation, close the browser window.

Save as **BaseCampWebPage.png** in the **WebPage** folder.

Spell checker!

It is a good idea to check your spelling. You can select a word with the Text tool and go to Text, Check Spelling.

If you have not set up a language then you will get this Spelling Setup window – check it is the same as Figure 18.13.

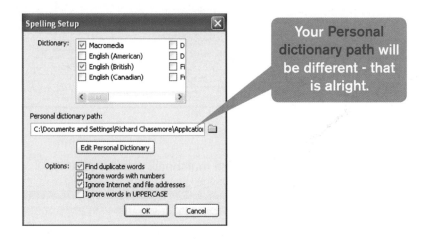

Figure 18.13: Spelling Setup

 Press OK.

When you run the Check Spelling function, you will get a Check Spelling window like Figure 18.14 if Fireworks finds a mistake. Select the correct spelling and choose Change.

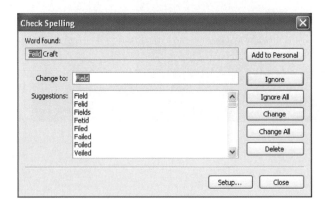

Figure 18.14: Check Spelling

The spell checker will even check your layer names, so it is very useful. It will tell you when it is complete, and you can then click OK to finish.

 Save your work as BaseCampWebPage.png in the WebPage folder when you are happy with the page.

Good Marks... ✓

You will get good marks if you:

- edit your images using tools and effects to enhance your message
- use images that will appeal to your target audience
- use design and effects to add impact and fun to your page
- save all the images in a suitable format and size for displaying on the Web
- get permission to use images and acknowledge copyright where necessary
- keep a record in the **Elements** table of all of the images you have used or created.

Bad Marks... ✗

You will lose marks if you:

- create a web page that contains spelling or grammar mistakes
- create a technically correct but boring web page
- create a messy-looking web page, or one that is too 'busy'
- omit any of the features that are specified in the brief.

Canvas Size

New size

↔	28	Centimeters	⌄	W: 793
↕	18	Centimeters	⌄	H: 510

Anchor:

Current size

↔ 793 pixels

↕ 510 pixels

OK   Cancel

Creating a checklist

Before you start designing the eportfolio, it would be a good idea to write a checklist of everything that needs to be included. When you come to do the Edexcel SPB, check the site, as a list may be provided for you.

Here is a sample list for this eportfolio:

Detailed project plan, with earlier version if necessary Evidence of monitoring (may be on the plan)	
Evidence of the elements you gathered before creating the products: • completed elements table.	
Evidence of ideas developed for the logo: • preliminary sketches of your logo, annotated to explain your design • image of logo, annotated to show feedback.	
Evidence of the birthday card: • photograph of mock-up showing dimensions • development showing use of grid and/or guides • image of the front and back of card, annotated to show feedback.	
Evidence of the Base Camp dollar: • annotated progression/development towards final image • final dollar note design, annotated to explain features • explanation of how the image would be prepared for printing.	
Evidence of web graphics: • at least one original graphic • thumbnails of original photograph(s), annotated to explain how you have edited them • finished webpage with banner and at least three images.	
Review of the project	

Don't forget to acknowledge your sources where you have used other people's images.

Remember that the requirements of each SPB will be different, so read the brief very carefully and make sure you include what is asked for and nothing else.

Drawing a structure chart

The next task is to draw a structure chart showing how the elements of the eportfolio will link together. The sketch below shows, amongst other things, that there will be three submenus under **Planning**: **Plan**, **Plan (Amended)** and **Elements table**.

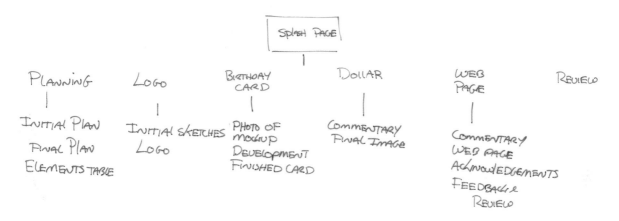

Figure 19.1: A structure chart

Designing the layout

Sketch out ideas on paper. (You don't have to include these sketches in the eportfolio.)

We will have two main features:

- A navigation bar along the top with drop-down menus. All pages will be accessible from every other page through the navigation bar. There will be a separate button on every page linking back to the home page.

- A column down the left-hand side, which will contain a commentary about the graphics in the main part of the screen.

Figure 19.2: A sketch of the eportfolio

We will have a splash page, which will look slightly different. In order to do this, we will create two templates in Dreamweaver, one for the splash page and one for all of the other pages. The navigation bar with its drop-down menus will be created in Fireworks and imported into Dreamweaver. The links can be set up in either Fireworks or Dreamweaver. (We will do this in Dreamweaver.)

This chapter will introduce you to Dreamweaver 8/MX 2004 and take you through the initial stages involved in creating a simple website. If you have an earlier version of Dreamweaver, the steps and screenshots are very similar.

Folder structure

When you set up a new site, you will be asked where on your computer you want it to be saved. It is therefore a good idea to create a suitable folder structure before creating a new site.

Each page on your site and each image you use will be a separate file. By the time you've created a website with many pages and images, there will be a lot of files; therefore you need to make sure they are well-organised from the start.

For any website, the main folders you will want are **HTML_files**, **Images**, **Library** and **Templates**.

HTML_files

Each page in your website will be an **HTML** file, and will go in this folder.

Images

Any image inserted on a web page is stored separately as an image file, and should be put in this folder. The image files used in the Base Camp eportfolio include **.jpg** and **.png** files.

Library

The library is not actually used in this book, but we'll create the folder anyway because it is good practice.

When you are creating your website, you can add various objects – such as images or paragraphs of text – to the library. This is useful for items that are used often, because if a library item is updated, every instance of this library item is also updated. Each item added to the library is given its own library file, which is stored in this folder.

Templates

As soon as you create a template, Dreamweaver will automatically create the **Templates** folder for you, so you won't need to create that. You can create templates in Dreamweaver in much the same way as in Word. Once the template is created, you can base subsequent pages on that template. All template files have the file extension **.dwt** and will be stored in this folder.

Creating the folders

You can create the folders using the **Files** panel in Dreamweaver. However, if you are completely new to Dreamweaver, it may be advisable to use Windows Explorer because you will be more familiar with it. We'll use the **Files** panel later.

Using Windows Explorer

To create the folders in Windows Explorer:

 Open Windows Explorer by right-clicking on the **Start** button and clicking **Explore** from the context menu that appears.

Figure 19.3: Opening Windows Explorer from the Start menu

 Navigate to your **BaseCampEportfolio** folder.

 Create three more folders in the **BaseCampEportfolio** folder, named **HTML_files**, **Images** and **Library**. You don't need to create the **Templates** folder yet because Dreamweaver will create it for you when you save your first template.

Your file structure should now look like this:

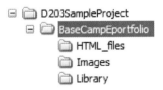

Figure 19.4: The file structure

 Close Windows Explorer. It's time to open Dreamweaver!

177

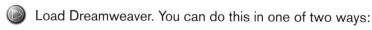

Creating a website in Dreamweaver

Load Dreamweaver. You can do this in one of two ways:

- *Either* double-click the Dreamweaver icon on your windows desktop

- *or* click **Start**, **Programs** then find the **Macromedia** folder and select **Macromedia Dreamweaver 8**.

If this is the first time you have opened Dreamweaver, it will ask you about workspace options.

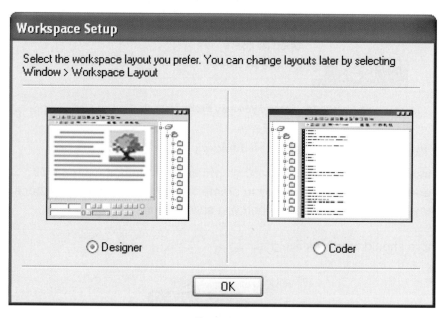

Figure 19.5

Choose **Designer** by making sure the first option button is selected, then click **OK**.

You will then see this window.

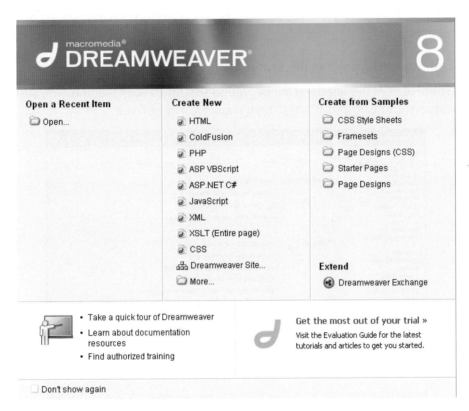

Figure 19.6

You don't want to see this **Start** page every time you open Dreamweaver, so click the box, in the bottom left of the screen, marked **Don't show again**. Click **OK** in the dialogue box that appears.

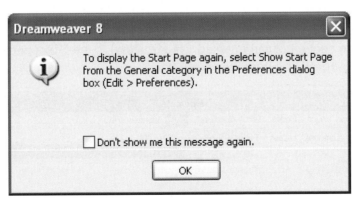

Figure 19.7

The green **Start** page will stay open until you choose an option from it. Don't choose anything yet – we will do that in a minute.

Changing workspace options

Let's make sure that the **Spelling dictionary** is set to **English (British)** instead of the default **English (American)**.

 Select **Edit**, **Preferences** from the **Menu** bar at the top of the screen.

 Select **General** from the left-hand list of categories. Make sure that the **Spelling dictionary** is set to **English (British)**, as shown in Figure 19.8.

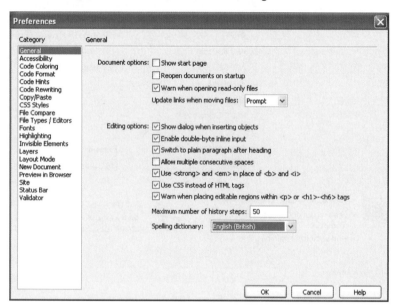

Figure 19.8

 Click **OK** to close the **Preferences** window.

Creating a new site

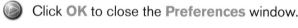 The green **Start** page should still be visible. Select the **Dreamweaver Site...** option near the bottom of the centre column (marked **Create New**). If the **Start** page is not visible, select **Site**, **Manage Sites** from the **Menu** bar.

Figure 19.9

The **Site Definition** window appears. By default, the **Basic** tab will be selected. This will take you through the wizard. We will not use the wizard, as it includes a lot of options that we just don't need at this stage.

Click the **Advanced** tab.

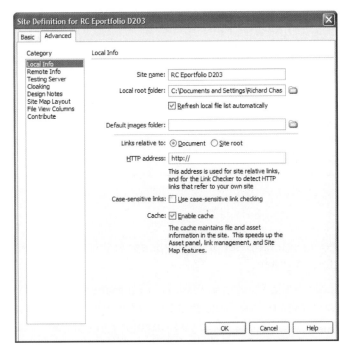

Figure 19.10: Site definition

Enter **RC Eportfolio D203** (or use your own initials) as the **Site name**.

Click the **Browse** icon next to the **Local root folder** and locate the **BaseCampEportfolio** folder that you just created. Click **Select**.

File Icon

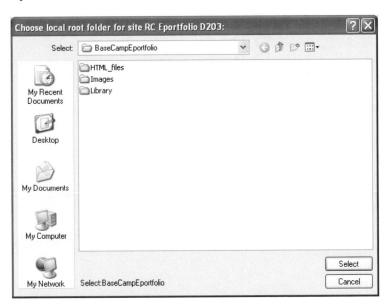

Figure 19.11: Selecting a local root folder for the site

You don't need to fill in any of the other options yet so just click **OK**.

We have now set up the website and we are ready to start adding web pages!

 Tip:

In Dreamweaver MX, the workspace will open with a new blank page called **Untitled-1** already created. You can leave this open for now.

The Files panel

Notice that all of the folders you have set up now appear in the **Files** panel. Anything associated with this site will be coloured green.

If your folders don't appear in the **Files** panel, make sure that you have **RC Eportfolio D203** and **Local View** selected as shown below. Note that this is the **Site Name**, which is not necessarily the same as the root folder name – it is up to you whether you choose to call them the same thing. Our root folder name is **BaseCampEportfolio**.

Figure 19.12: The Files panel

You can easily change folder names, add new folders or delete files using the **Files** panel in the same way as you would using Windows Explorer.

We have successfully set up a new site. In the next chapter, we will create the two templates we need.

Chapter 20 – Creating Templates

The web pages for **RC Eportfolio D203** will be based on templates so that they all have the same design and layout.

The key to a professional-looking website is to use a clean, simple template and to base every page on it. The navigation bar is also included on the template, so that, whichever page you are on, you have access to the same navigation buttons. This not only gives the website coherence and continuity, it also makes it easy for people to browse your website without getting lost!

Our design has a splash page, which will be based on a different template from the other pages. The major difference is that it will not contain a navigation bar – just a link to enter the site. We will start by creating this template.

Creating a new template

You can create a template from scratch or an existing page can be converted into a template. We'll create a basic page and then later save it as a template.

 Select **File**, **New** from the **Menu** bar.

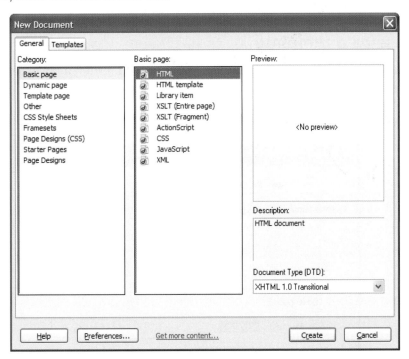

Figure 20.1: The New Document window

You could create a template page by selecting **HTML Template** from the **Basic Page** list. This would achieve the same result as saving the basic page as a template later.

 Make sure **Basic Page** is selected in the **Category** list and **HTML** is selected in the second list. Click **Create**.

Figure 20.2: The new blank page appears

Saving a page as a template

Remember – you've opened a new page, but it is not yet saved. When a file is saved, it will appear in the **Files** panel. We'll save the page now as a template.

 Select **File**, **Save as Template** from the **Menu** bar.

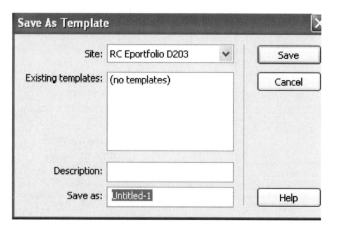

Figure 20.3: Saving a page as a template

 Set **Save as** to **SplashTemplate** and click **Save**.

> ### Important Note:
>
> Although you didn't specify where Dreamweaver should save the file, it will automatically create a **Templates** folder and put it in there. If you had created the **Templates** folder along with the others, it would have found that and saved the file in there.

The template may not yet be shown in the **Files** panel – you might need to refresh it first.

 In the **Files** panel, click the **Refresh** icon. Click the **+** sign to open the **Templates** folder if it is closed.

Refresh Icon

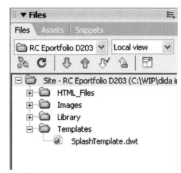

Figure 20.4: The SplashTemplate file appears in the Files panel

Tables

You've probably come across tables in Microsoft Word, where they are used to store data in columns and rows. In Dreamweaver, tables can be used to store columns and rows of data, but their main use is as a layout tool.

By using a large table, the size of the whole web page, you can adjust the columns and rows to divide up the page into sections.

A large table, the width of the whole page, will be the basis of our template.

The Insert bar

Whenever you want to insert anything, such as a table, an image, or a navigation bar, you will use the **Insert** bar. This is located at the top of the screen, just below the main menu bar.

Figure 20.5: The Insert bar

There are two different views of the **Insert** bar. The one which appears when you first open Dreamweaver is the one shown above; we will now change this to show tabs.

 Click where it says **Common** on the **Insert** bar, then select **Show as Tabs** from the menu that appears.

Figure 20.6

185

The **Insert** bar now appears as shown in Figure 20.7.

Figure 20.7

Tip:

To revert to the original view, click the **Options** icon in the top right of the **Insert** bar and select **Show as Menu** from the list.

We'll leave the **Insert** bar looking like this.

Important Note:

If you want to know what any of the icons are on the **Insert** bar, just hold the mouse over the icon for a few seconds: a **Tool tip** will appear with the name of the icon.

Inserting a table

Table Icon

- Make sure the cursor is in the top left of the page (it will be unless you've moved it); this is where we want to insert the table.

- Click the **Table** icon on the **Insert bar** (it is under the **Common** tab, which should already be selected). The **Table** dialogue box appears.

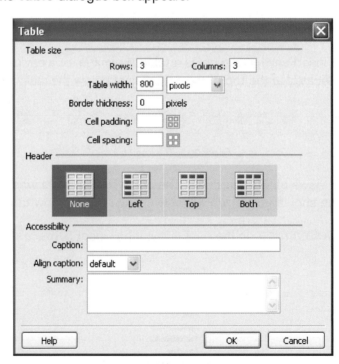

Figure 20.8: The Table dialogue box

Tip:

Most sites use a width of about 800 pixels. At this size, each page of your site will fit onto most screens without users having to scroll across. Some sites are as narrow as 600 pixels – this means that even people with relatively small screens can view a page without scrolling, but you can't fit as much on a page. **www.payne-gallway.co.uk** uses a width of 600 pixels. **www.bbc.co.uk** uses just less than 800.

▶ Fill in the **Table** dialogue box, as shown in Figure 20.8, with **3** rows and **3** columns. Enter the width as **800 pixels** and specify a value of **0** for the border. This creates an invisible border.

▶ Click **OK**.

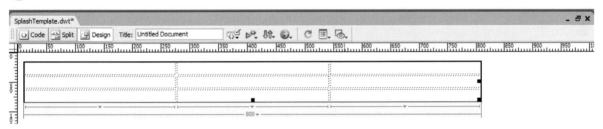

Figure 20.9: Inserting a new table

The table appears as shown above. It will need adjusting later on.

Selecting cells, rows and tables

The table in the screenshot above is selected – as yours probably is, because you've just created it. You can tell that it is selected, because it has a solid black border and small black handles around it. It also has green lines and text indicating the width of the table in pixels.

▶ Click away from the table to deselect it. The handles and green lines will disappear.

▶ Now click in the middle of the table. Look at the text at the bottom left of the page:

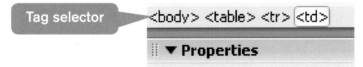

Figure 20.10: The Tag selector

These are called **tags**, and the area they are in is called the **Tag selector**. Clicking on one of the tags here will select the object it represents.

- Clicking **<td>** (short for **table data**) will select the **cell** that the cursor is in.
- Clicking **<tr>** (short for **table row**) will select the **row** the cursor is in.
- Clicking **<table>** will select the **table** the cursor is in.

187

⊙ Click each of these tags in turn and watch the black border highlight different parts of the table. This is the easiest way to select parts of a table.

The Properties inspector

At the bottom of the screen is the **Properties inspector**, similar to the one in Fireworks.

⊙ If you can't see the **Properties inspector**, select **Window**, **Properties** from the **Menu** bar. If the panel is collapsed, just click the small black arrow to the left of where it says **Properties**.

Figure 20.11: The Properties inspector

 Tip:

If your **Properties inspector** is smaller than the one above, you might need to expand yours. To do this, just click the small arrow in the bottom right of the **Properties inspector**.

⊙ Select the table you've just created, by clicking the **<table>** tag.

The table properties appear in the **Properties inspector**. You'll learn more about these properties in a minute.

⊙ Look at the properties of a cell and row by selecting them and viewing them in the **Properties inspector**.

Inserting and deleting rows and columns

Adding or deleting the last row or column

You can add or delete the bottom row or right-hand column simply by changing the number of rows and columns in the table properties (in the **Properties inspector**).

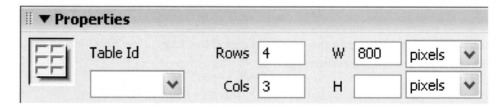

Figure 20.12: Changing the number of rows and columns

Make sure the **table** is selected. Change the number of rows to **4** using the **Properties inspector**.

Tip:

When changing properties in the **Properties inspector**, you need to either tab out of a cell or press **Enter** for the changes to take effect.

Tip:

Another way to add a row is to place the cursor in the last cell in a table and press the **Tab** key.

Inserting or deleting a row or column in the middle of a table

Right-click in the top left cell in the table.

Select **Table**, **Delete Row** from the context menu that appears.

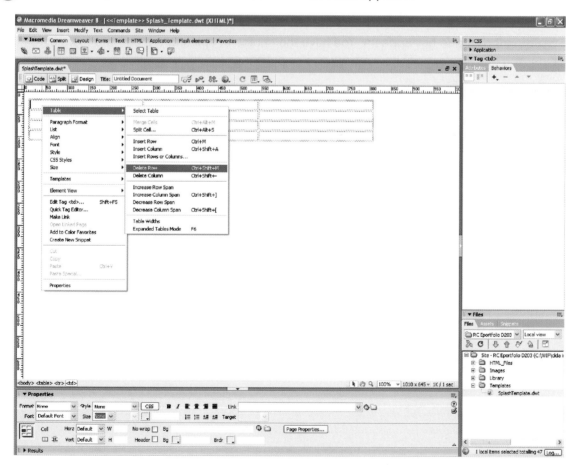

Figure 20.13: Deleting a row

Use the same method to delete another row and one of the columns.

The table should now have two rows and two columns.

Merging and splitting cells

You can easily merge and split cells, so that the number of rows and columns varies across the table. The quickest way to merge and split cells is to use the icons in the **Properties inspector**.

Merging

Merge Cells Icon

▶ Select the entire first row in the table. Click the **Merge Cells** icon in the **Properties inspector**.

The cells are merged, and there's only one column in the first row.

Splitting

Split Cells Icon

▶ Select the left cell in row **2**.

▶ Click the **Split Cells** icon in the **Properties inspector**.

The **Split Cell** dialogue box appears. You have the choice of splitting the cell into rows or columns. You can also specify how many rows or columns.

▶ Enter the settings shown in Figure 20.14, and then click **OK**.

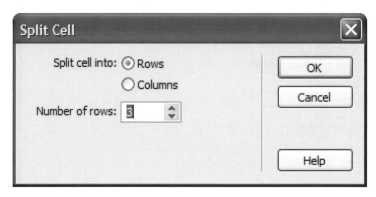

Figure 20.14: Splitting cells

The cell is split into three cells vertically.

Figure 20.15: The result of splitting cells

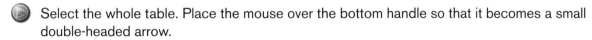

Resizing cells and tables

Resizing a table

The table should at least fill the visible area on the screen, so we need to make it much longer.

- Select the whole table. Place the mouse over the bottom handle so that it becomes a small double-headed arrow.

- Click and drag the handle down so that the table is about **600** pixels (the height will be shown in the **Properties inspector**). Release the mouse when you're happy with the size.

> **Tip:**
>
> You don't need to worry that a table cell won't be big enough to fit an object because the table will always grow to fit whatever you put in.

Resizing cells

To resize cells, just click and drag the table border between the cells. Place the mouse over the border you want to resize so that the pointer becomes an arrow. Click and drag the border to where you want it, then release it.

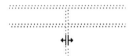

Figure 20.16: Resizing rows and columns

- Click and drag the borders so that your table looks like the one below. Resizing tables isn't an exact science in Dreamweaver; it sometimes takes a bit of trial and error – and a bit of patience! The large cell needs to be about 600 pixels wide. Make sure that the table is still 600 pixels tall afterwards.

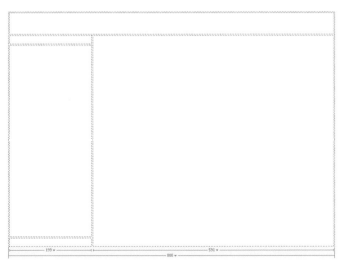

Figure 20.17: Using a table to lay out the page

Eliminating borders

In this website we don't want white gaps between the cells.

⊙ Make sure that the entire table is selected by clicking on the **\<table\>** tag.

⊙ Set the **CellSpace** and **Border** properties to **0**.

Figure 20.18

Saving the template

It is very important to save your work regularly.

⊙ To save the template, click on **File**, **Save** on the **Menu** (or press **Ctrl-S** as a shortcut).

⊙ Click **OK** in the warning window, if one appears. You will create some editable regions soon!

Inserting a background image

We are going to put an image on the splash screen, with some text over it. We have to be careful to size the image so it fits well. You may need to save it from Fireworks several times at different image sizes.

⊙ Click in the large, bottom right cell of the table.

⊙ In the **Properties inspector**, change **Horz** to **Left** and **Vert** to **Top**. Your cursor will jump to the top left of the cell.

Figure 20.19: Changing the cell alignment using the Properties inspector

Exporting the logo image from Fireworks

▶ Open Fireworks and load **BaseCampLogo.png** from your **Logo\Artwork** folder.

▶ Go to **File, Export Wizard**.

▶ Choose **Select an export format** and click **Continue**.

▶ In the **Choose Destination** box, select **The web**. Click **Continue**.

▶ In the next window, click **Exit**.

▶ In the **Image Preview** window, choose between **.jpg** and **.gif**. I went for **.jpg** as I had a shadow on the text; look at the preview to make your choice. If you don't have a shadow, choose **.gif**.

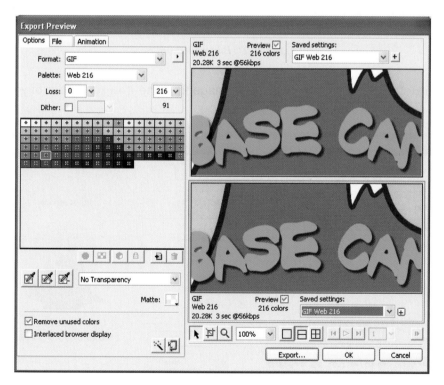

Figure 20.20: Optimising the image

▶ Click the **File** tab in the **Image Preview** window. Change the width and height to **550** pixels so it will fit into the web page box.

▶ Press **Export** and navigate to your **BaseCampEportfolio\Images** folder. Set the **File name** to **BaseCampLogoBackground** and click **Export**.

▶ Click the **Dreamweaver** tab at the bottom of the screen to bring back Dreamweaver.

Background URL

🔘 Make sure the cursor is in the large right-hand cell.

🔘 Click the **Background URL of Cell** button in the **Properties inspector** (see Figure 20.21).

Press this folder icon (**Background URL of cell**).

Figure 20.21: Background URL

🔘 Select the **BaseCampLogoBackground** image from the **Images** folder of your website. Click **OK**.

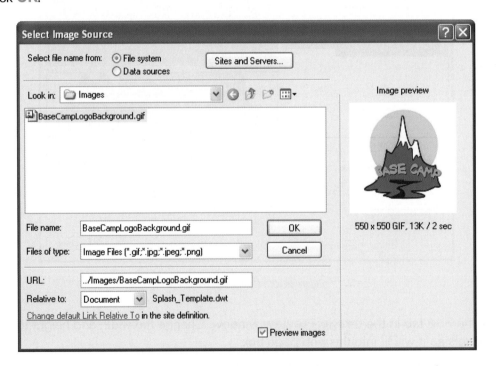

Figure 20.22: Inserting the background logo image

Changing the background colour

▶ Click in the top row of the table and select it by clicking the **<tr>** tag.

▶ Select the **Background Color** box marked **Bg** in the **Properties inspector**.

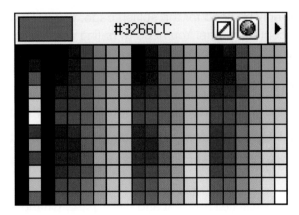

Figure 20.23

▶ Use the **Color Dropper** by clicking inside your logo to select the blue colour of the mountain.

▶ Shade the other cells as shown in Figure 20.24.

Figure 20.24

Tip:

Colours chosen from the palette are **Web Safe**, meaning they will look the same on any browser. A blend of colours, on the other hand, such as from the **Colour Picker**, is not guaranteed.

Defining editable regions

When you base a web page on this template, any areas that have not been specified as editable regions will be locked. This means that you will not be able to change those areas that you have not made 'editable'.

Although this template will only be used for the splash page, you will save and edit a second version of it to use for the content pages. You need to define some of the cells as editable regions so that content can be added to them.

▶ Click in the large cell on the left.

▶ Go to the **Menu** bar and choose **Insert**, **Template Objects**, **Editable Region**.

▶ In the **New Editable Region** window, name the region **Commentary**, and click **OK**.

▶ Select the surrounding **<td>** element and, in the **Properties inspector**, change **Horz** to **Center** and **Vert** to **Top**.

▶ Repeat the steps in the small cell above it and call it **Title**. Change the **Horz** and **Vert** settings to **Center**, **Middle**.

▶ Repeat this process to define an editable region for the main window, calling it **Description Text**. Change the **Horz** and **Vert** settings to **Left**, **Top**.

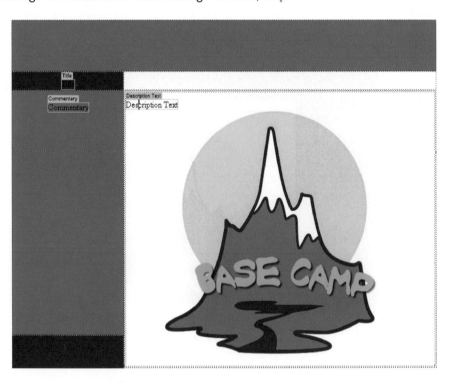

Figure 20.25: Adding editable regions

Setting page properties in the template

To keep all the pages looking consistent, we can set text styles for the different editable regions. We can also set a text style for the entire page, using the **Page Properties** button in the **Properties inspector** or using **Modify**, **Page Properties**.

 Click the **Page Properties** button.

 Select **Arial**, **Helvetica**, **sans-serif** as the **Page font**. Your **Page Properties** dialogue will look like Figure 20.26. Press **OK**.

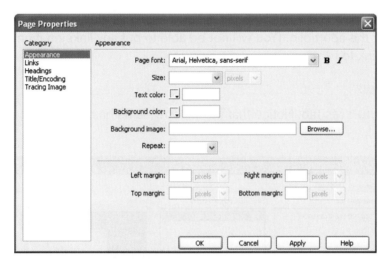

Figure 20.26: Setting page properties

Setting text styles in the template

 Highlight the text in the **Title** cell. Change the font size to **24 pixels**, and the colour to the gold colour of the logo.

 Make the **Commentary** text **Bold**, **light grey**, font size **18 pixels**.

 Set the **Description Text** region's text to the dark blue of the logo, font size **16 pixels**.

 You have set up three different styles, which you can use in any of the pages based on this template. Click the **Style** box in the **Properties inspector** to see them.

Figure 20.27

Save the template again and close the file.

Creating a web page using a template

Now that you have created your template in Dreamweaver, you can use it to very quickly create the splash page for the eportfolio. (You will not be able to put any links on it until you have created a page to link to.)

 Click **File**, **New**.

 Select the **Templates** tab. Notice that the window name has changed to **New from Template**.

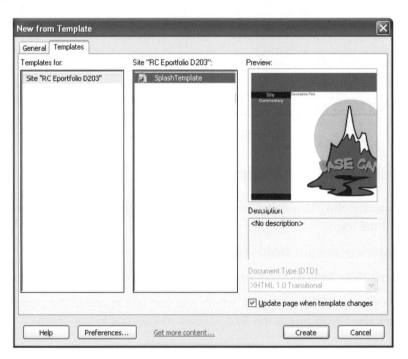

Figure 20.28: New from Template

 Select **SplashTemplate** and click **Create**.

 You should see a new page with the template design. Try changing a part of the template that you did not specify as editable. It will be locked.

Adding text

 Click in the **Commentary** cell with the grey text and add your name, candidate number, school or college name and centre number.

> ! **Tip:**
>
> You can press **Shift-Enter** for a **soft return**.

 Highlight the **Title** text and replace it with **Splash Page**.

 In the **Description** text box, type the text shown in Figure 20.29.

 Format the text as **Arial**, **36 pixels**. Choose the green colour of the logo.

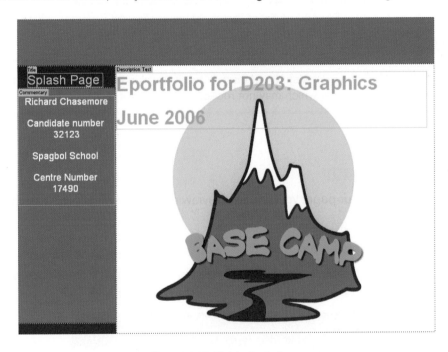

Figure 20.29: Finished splash page

Saving your splash page

Saving a splash page (or the home page, if you do not have a splash page) is slightly different from saving a regular page. Firstly it must be given a particular name – **index.html** – and secondly it must be saved in the root folder of your website rather than in the **HTML_Files** folder. This is because nearly all servers look for a file called **index.html** in the root folder. If they can't find it, your website cannot be displayed.

 Click **File**, **Save**.

⊚ Enter the filename **index.html**.

Figure 20.30: Saving the splash page as index.html

It is important to remember the extension **.html** on the end of the filename. This makes it most accessible to other web browsers, which may not recognise the default **.htm** extension.

⊚ Click **Save**.

Previewing a web page

Now that you have saved your page, you can try previewing it in a web browser such as Internet Explorer.

⊚ If you have Internet Explorer, press the **F12** key.

⊚ If you have a different browser, select **File**, **Preview in Browser** from the main menu. If the browser you want isn't listed there, select **Edit Browser List**.

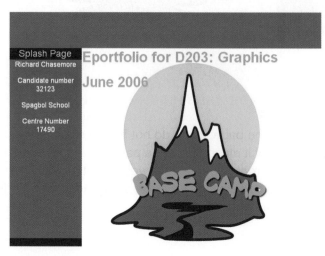

Figure 20.31: Previewing the page in a browser

Naming your web page

You can specify the text that appears in the blue bar at the top of the web page window.

In the **Document** bar, name the page **Splash Page**.

Figure 20.32: Naming a web page

▶ Save the page and view it again in a browser by pressing **F12**.

▶ Close the browser. When you are happy with your page, save and close the file.

That's the first page done. Now we need to create the content pages.

The content pages

You should make a list of every page that you are going to create, and the graphics, photographs, scanned images, text or pdf files that you are going to put on each one.

Here is a list of what needs to go into this eportfolio.

Page name	Images	Done
Splash page	BaseCampLogo.png optimized as BaseCampLogoBackground.gif.	
HomePage.html	None.	
PlanInitial.html	PlanInitial.doc.	
PlanFinal.html	PlanAmended.doc.	
Elements.html	Elements table Elements.doc.	
LogoSketches.html	Scanned sketch of design Logosketches.jpg in DownloadedImages.	
Logo.html	BaseCampLogoV1.png optimized as BaseCampLogoV1.gif. BaseCampLogo.png optimized as BaseCampLogo.jpg.	
CardPhoto.html	Photo of card, CardMockup.jpg saved for web.	
CardDevelopment.html	Old versions of Card.png, showing progress of development. Optimised as gifs for the web.	
CardFinished.html	Card.png optimized as Card.gif.	
DollarCommentary.html	Old versions of Dollar.png, optimised as jpgs for the web.	
DollarFinal.html	Dollar.png optimized as Dollar.jpg.	
WebPageCommentary.html	Screenshot of Explorer showing thumbnail images saved as ExplorerThumbnails.jpg, optimized as Thumbnails.jpg. Montage.png optimized as MontageWeb.jpg. Screenshot of Webpage.html when mouse pointer rolls over Jumper, optimized as JumperRollover.jpg. Original and manipulated image of CatamaranSailing.jpg. optimized as CatamaranWeb.jpg and CatBlur.jpg.	
WebPage.html	BaseCampWebPage.png exported as html and images.	
WebPageAcknowledgements.html	None.	
WebPageReview.html	None.	
Review.html	None.	

All of the images have already been created and saved in your folder structure. Some or all of them may need to be reduced in size or made web-ready, and all the images that you are going to use should be saved into the **BaseCampEportfolio\Images** folder.

Creating a template for the content pages

We will start by creating a second template, which will be similar to the splash page template but will contain a navigation bar and a separate button to link back to the home page.

- In Dreamweaver, click **File**, **Open Recent** to see your recent documents. Open **SplashTemplate.dwt**.

- Click in the large main cell. In the **Properties inspector**, delete the **Background URL**.

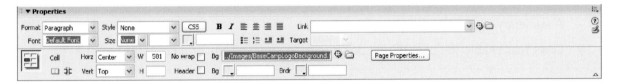

Figure 21.1: Removing the background image

- Change the text in the **Description Text** cell to **Main Content**.

- Change the font in the **Commentary** cell to **14 pixels**, not **Bold**. Make it the dark blue of the logo.

- Click in the cell and change the background colour of the commentary bar so that dark blue text will be clearly legible.

Figure 21.2: The main template

- Save this template as **MainTemplate** and close it.

The home page

We will start by creating the home page.

> Edexcel specifies that this should contain the following:
>
> - Your name, registration number and your centre name and number
> - Date completed
> - A clear description of the purpose of the eportfolio
> - A summary of what can be found inside
> - Links that enable the user to drill down (e.g. to menu pages or a contents page).

⊚ Create a new page based on **MainTemplate**.

Some of the information can be copied from the splash page.

⊚ Open **index.html**.

⊚ Copy the text and paste it to the new page.

⊚ Add new text to complete the page.

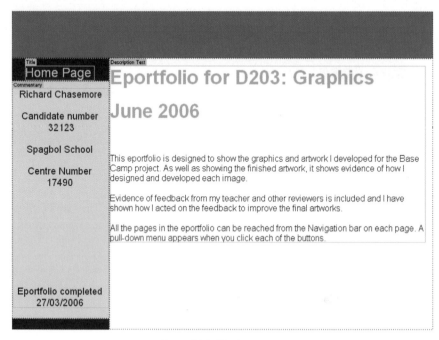

Figure 21.3: The home page

⊚ Press **F12** to view your page in Internet Explorer. You will be prompted to save the page
– save it as **HomePage.html** in your **HTML_files** folder.

⊚ Close this page. The navigation bar will be added later.

The project plan pages

 Create a new page based on **MainTemplate**.

 In Word, open your original plan, which you should have saved in your **ProjectDocumentation** folder.

Tip:

You will probably need to reduce the text size to **9** or **10** point before pasting it into your web page, to make it fit.

You may find your columns change size. This is a common problem in Dreamweaver. Sometimes the problem sorts itself out, and sometimes the columns will look different in a browser. Basically you should try to avoid placing text and images which are too wide for the given cell.

 Copy the whole table. Then paste it into the white box containing the text **Main Content**. Add headings and a commentary.

 In the **Title** box in the **Insert** bar, give the page a title: **Initial Plan**.

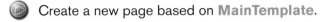

Initial Plan

Commentary

This was my initial plan. I saved a second version so that I could show the original plan in the eportfolio. I made notes of changes etc on version2.

Task	Task Name	Subtask	Time allowed	Start Date	End Date	Home/Class	Notes
1	Plan the project	Read the project brief	1 day	9 sep	9 sep	class	
		Create an organised folder structure for the project files	1 day	11 sep	11 sep	class	
		Produce a plan listing individual tasks, subtasks, estimated completion dates etc.	1 day	16 sep	16 sep	class	
	CHECKPOINT	*Check plan with teacher*				class	
2	Create logo	Collect stimulus material for cooperate image, logo	2 weeks	9 Sep	23 Sep	Home/class	
		Sketch some ideas	2 weeks	18 Sep	24 Sep	home	
		Scan the sketches to include in eportfolio	2 weeks			class	
		Create the logo				class	
		Get feedback				class	
		Make changes if necessary				class	
3	Birthday card	Gather stimulus material					
		Make mock-up and take photograph					
		Start card and take screenshot showing early version with grid					
		Complete both sides of card					
		Get feedback					
		Make changes if necessary					
	CHECKPOINT	*Check work with teacher*					
4	Web page	*(fill in subtasks)*					
5	Create eportfolio	*(fill in subtasks)*					

Figure 21.4: The Initial Plan page

 View your page in a browser.

- Save this page as **PlanInitial.html** in your **HTML_files** folder.

- Create a new page for your amended plan, and paste in the plan from your Word document. Don't forget to add a commentary, and give the page a title in the **Title** box. Save it as **PlanFinal.html** in the **HTML_files** folder.

- Create a new page for your **Elements** table, and paste in the table from your Word document. Don't forget to add a commentary and give the page a title in the **Title** box. Save it as **ElementsTable.html**.

Elements Table

This is my Elements table which contains details of all the primary and secondary sources I used.

ELEMENTS TABLE

Image(file name)	Primary/ Secondary Source	Bitmap/ Vector/ Combination	Description	Source Details	Where used	Permission (how obtained if required)
CatmaranSailing.jpg	S	Bitmap	Girl sailing a catamaran	www.acornadventure.co.uk	Base CampWeb page montage	Emailed photographer
ArdecheRapids.jpg	S	Bitmap	Canoeing	www.acornadventure.co.uk	Base CampWeb page montage	Emailed photographer
Climbing.jpg	S	Bitmap	Climbing	www.acornadventure.co.uk	Base CampWeb page montage	Emailed photographer
Abseiling.jpg	S	Bitmap	Abseiling	www.acornadventure.co.uk	Base CampWeb page montage	Emailed photographer

Figure 21.5: The Elements table

The Logo Sketches page

Next, we will create the **LogoSketches** page.

- Open a new page based on **MainTemplate**. Save it as **LogoSketches.html** in the **HTML_files** folder.

- Start Fireworks, if it isn't already running.

- In Fireworks, load the sketch you scanned in during Chapter 7 (it should be in your **Logo\ Scans** folder, saved as a **png** file).

- Select **File**, **Export Wizard**. Work through the wizard, following the same process you did when exporting the background logo (see Chapter 20). Save the file as **LogoSketches.gif** in your **BaseCampEportfolio\Images** folder.

Dreamweaver has an option to prompt you for accessibility information each time you add certain types of object to a web page. This exercise assumes that these options have been turned off (we'll set the accessibility information manually), but you might like to turn them back on for your own projects.

- For now, in Dreamweaver, select **Edit**, **Preferences** from the **Menu** bar. Select **Accessibility** and untick the top group of options. Press **OK**.

- Highlight the white **Main Content** text box.

- Click the **Image** button on the **Insert** toolbar. Navigate to the **LogoSketches.gif** image and press **OK**.

Image Icon

Your image will appear on the page. You can add some commentary, and a title. Don't forget to give the page a name in the **Title** box.

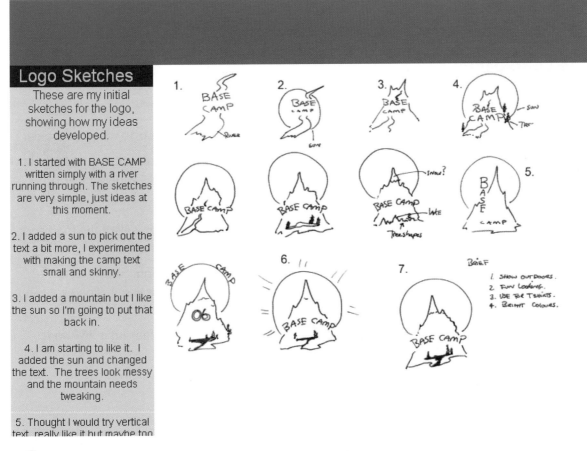

Figure 21.6: Logo sketches

 Tip:

You could also add any logos that you took inspiration from, which should already be in your **Logo\Reference** folder.

Accessibility

This refers to the practice of making web pages more readable to blind or partially sighted people. Special software can read out the text, but images need to be described in words when the web page is created. You can specify **alternate text**, which briefly describes the image and will be read out.

This text appears when the mouse pointer passes over the image.

Tip:

Accessibility is a feature that is specified in the marking scheme for the SPB and it will be obvious to the moderator if it has been done or not!

▶ Select the **LogoSketches** image. In the **Properties inspector**, type **Logo Sketches** in the **Alt** box.

▶ Save your page, check it in a browser and then close it.

The Logo page

Preparing the images

▶ Back in Fireworks, open the **BaseCampLogo.png** image from the **Logo\Artwork** folder.

▶ From the **File** menu, click **Export Wizard**. Go through the same process as you did to save your sketches. Click the **File** tab and make the image size **250 pixels** wide and high.

▶ Save the image as **LogoSmall.gif** in the **Images** folder.

▶ To save a greyscale image, make sure **BaseCampLogo.png** is open, select the logo and from the **Menu** bar click **Commands**, **Creative**, **Convert to Greyscale**.

▶ Now export this image as a **JPEG**, making it **400 pixels** wide and high. Save it as **LogoGreyscale.jpg** in the **Images** folder. Close the logo without saving it, since we want to keep the colour version.

▶ Finally, export an early version of your logo as either a **.gif** or a **.jpg**, making it **250** wide and high.

Inserting the images on the web page

▶ Return to Dreamweaver.

▶ Create a new page based on **MainTemplate**. Save it as **Logo.html** in the **HTML_files** folder.

When you have several different images to show on a page, it is a good idea to insert a table within the main content area, with a cell for each image you want to include, and perhaps a cell at the bottom for acknowledgements. This gives you greater control over where each object is placed on the page and also stops objects moving unpredictably in the browser!

We will insert a table to hold the images and acknowledgements.

- Click in the **Main Content** box and delete the text.

- Click the **Insert Table** button to insert a table of **2** rows and **2** columns, **600** pixels wide. Click **OK**.

Insert Table Icon

- Select the two cells in the second row, and click the **Merge cells** button.

- Click in the top left-hand cell.

- Click the **Image** button on the **Insert** toolbar. Navigate to the **BaseCampLogoV1.gif** image (or whatever you called your early version) and press **OK**.

- Insert the final logo image in the right-hand cell.

- Insert the greyscale logo in the second row of the table.

You can add some commentary, and finish the page off. Don't forget to give the page a name in the **Title** box. It will probably look best if you change the **Horiz** property of each **<td>** to **Center**.

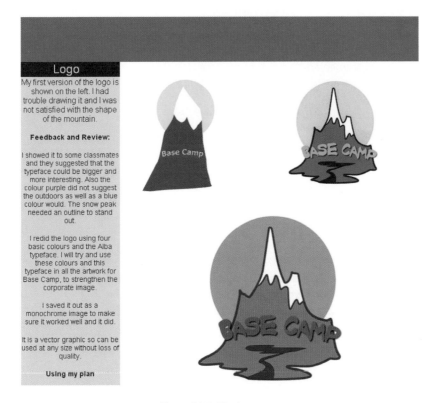

Figure 21.7: The Logo page

- Save your page, check in a browser, then close it.

The birthday card pages

No new techniques are used here. The photograph has been manipulated before being placed in the eportfolio – you can have a go at this!

Figure 21.8

Important Note:

Chapter 22 explains how to create the navigation bar you can see running across the top of Figure 21.8. Don't worry about this for now.

The sample SPB specifies that you should show how you used a grid, and how you developed the card. Be sure to pay attention to the commentary, which will earn you many marks!

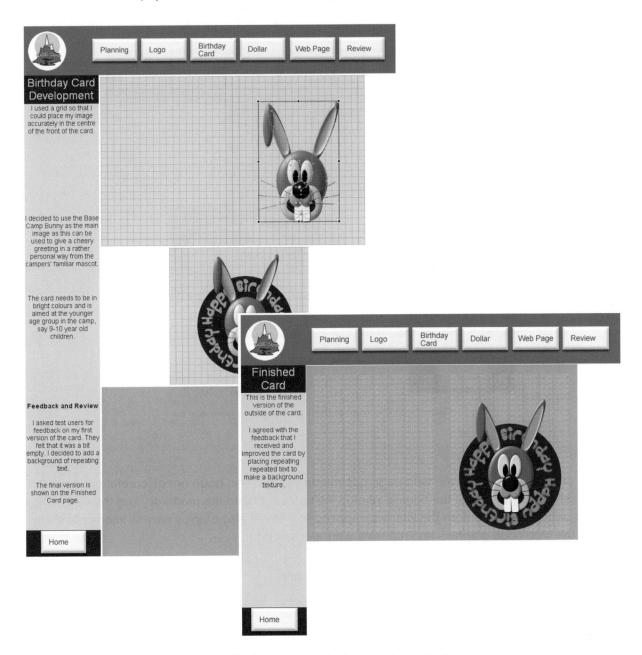

Figure 21.9: Birthday card pages after insertion of navigation bar

The dollar note pages

These pages are left as an exercise for you to complete. No new techniques are needed – you will need to optimise all the images you are going to use, and save them in the **Images** folder.

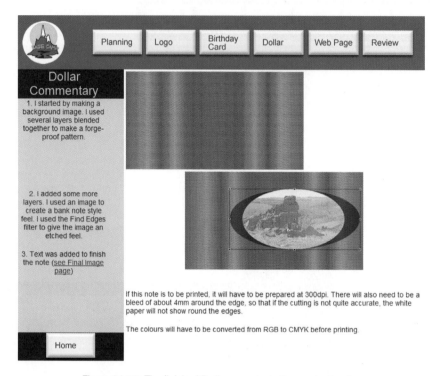

Figure 21.10: The finished Dollar page including navigation bar

The Base Camp web pages

First of all, we will create the web page commentary page. This page needs careful planning. It will show thumbnails of the original photos we used to create the montage, and then show how the montage looked before the filter was applied to it. It will also display several images to show how the web page graphics and rollovers were developed.

Preparing the new page for the commentary

 Create a new page based on **MainTemplate**.

 Insert the page title **Web Page Commentary** and save the file as **WebPageCommentary.html**.

We will insert a table to hold the images and acknowledgements.

Insert Table Icon

Click in the **Main Content** box, and click the **Insert Table** button to insert a table of **5** rows and **2** columns, **600** pixels wide. Click **OK**.

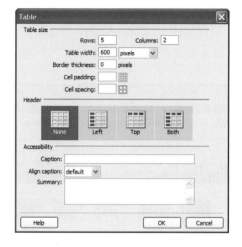

Figure 21.11: Inserting a table within the main cell

Select the two cells in the first row, and click the **Merge cells** button.

Merge Cells
Icon

Preparing the images

In Windows Explorer, navigate to the folder that contains all your downloaded images.

Click the **View** button to display them as thumbnails. You want to capture a screenshot of all the photos used in the montage and on the web page, so you may need to move some images to another folder temporarily.

Take a screenshot of the thumbnail images.

Create a new file in Fireworks, accept the canvas size and paste in the screenshot from the clipboard. Crop it so it looks something like Figure 21.12.

Figure 21.12: Thumbnails of original images

Use the **Export Wizard** to optimise the image for the web and reduce the image size to about **550 pixels wide**. Export it as **Thumbnails.jpg** and save it in your **Images** folder.

Take a look at Figure 21.13. You need to optimise, size and save each of the images shown.

Place the images and text on your web page in appropriate cells.

 Tip:

You can look at the website **www. payne-gallway.co.uk/didaD203/eportfolio** to see how I did mine. You can add more rows and show other development work, your banner, etc.

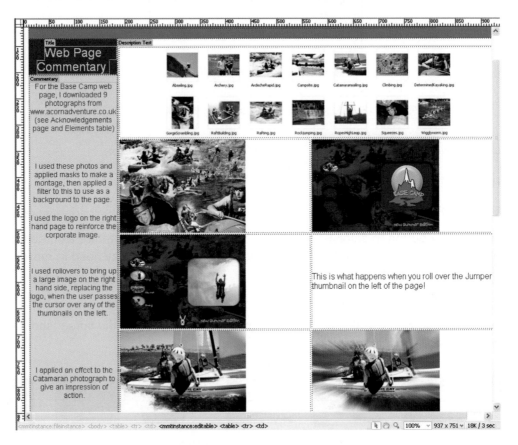

Figure 21.13: Finished web page commentary page

 View the page in a browser then save and close it.

The Base Camp web page

You have already created the web page in Fireworks. All you need to do is export it to Dreamweaver. When we add the navigation bar, we will make it open the web page in a separate window. Closing the window will return the user to the page they were on.

 Open Fireworks if it is not already open, and open **BaseCampWebPage.png**.

On the **Menu** bar, click **File**, **Export Wizard**.

Make sure the **Select an export format** option is selected and press **Continue**.

- Check **Single image file** and press **Continue**.

- Choose **The web**. We need to make sure the eportfolio is as small as possible in megabytes. Press **Continue**.

- Press **Exit**.

The file size is already **800 pixels** wide so that is fine. We need to export as a **.jpg** because of all of our fine bitmap images.

- Make sure that the **Format** is set to **JPEG**.

- Click on **Export**.

- Navigate to your **HTML_Files** folder in **BaseCampEportfolio**. Check the **Put images in subfolder** box, and use the **Browse** button to put them into your **BaseCampEportfolio\ Images** folder. Make sure the file name is **BaseCampWebPage.html**.

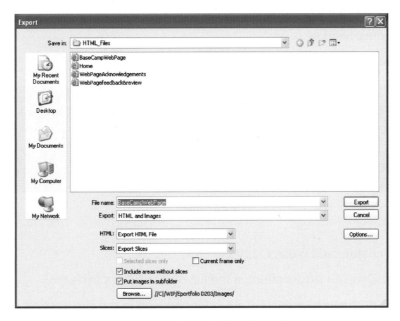

Figure 21.14: Exporting from Fireworks

- Click **Export**.

- Return to Dreamweaver, and open **BaseCampWebPage.html**.

- There it is! Click on **F12** to preview in a browser– does everything work OK? Check the rollovers.

- Save and close your **BaseCampWebPage**.

The Review page

This page is up to you! Before you start work on this, refer to the Edexcel SPB website for this module, where you will find very helpful guidance on the **Review** page.

Now we can create the navigation bar in Fireworks.

Load Fireworks and create a new canvas with a **Width** of **800 Pixels**, a **Height** of **100 Pixels**, a **Resolution** of **72 Pixels/Inch**, and the **Canvas color** set to a **Custom** medium or dark blue.

Right-click the canvas and select **Insert New Button**. The **Button Editor** will automatically open so that you can create your button.

Draw a vector rectangle and use the **Eye Candy 4000LE Bevel Boss filter** (**effect**) to make it look like a button.

Text Icon

Scale Icon

Use the **Text** tool to write the text **Birthday Card** on it in size **16**. This is the most characters you will have to put on any of the buttons.

Select the button and use the **Scale** tool to make it taller if necessary. (The text will need to go on two lines.) You need to get six buttons across the navigation bar, and also the Base Camp logo, so you will have to keep the buttons and text quite small.

Add a subtle drop shadow.

Change the text to **Planning** for the first button.

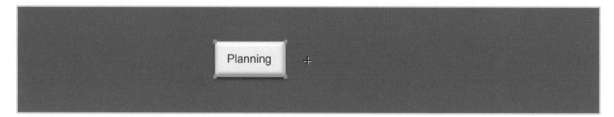

Figure 22.1

Go to the **Over** state and press **Copy Up Graphic**.

Switch off the **Drop Shadow** effect in the list of **live filters** (**effects**).

Edit Live Filters Icon

Click the **Edit and arrange live filters** (**effects**) icon in the **Properties inspector** to edit the **Bevel Boss** effect.

Click the **Lighting** tab and drag the highlight down very slightly to make the button look depressed. Press **OK**.

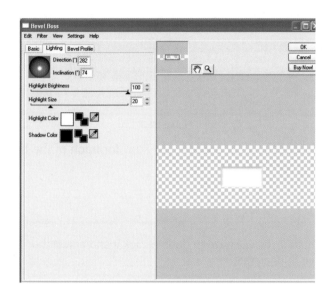

Figure 22.2

▶ Click the **Down** state tab and press **Copy Over Graphic**.

▶ Select the vector rectangle and, in the **Properties inspector**, make the background light grey.

▶ Click the **Over While Down** state tab and press **Copy Down Graphic**. (We don't need to change the button's appearance for this state.)

▶ Click **Done**.

The button automatically has a slice inserted.

▶ Save your work in the **WebPage** folder as **NavBar.png**.

▶ Press **F12** to view it in the browser. Close and return to Fireworks.

Tip:

If you need to edit the button, double-click it to enter the **Button Editor**. If the down state doesn't work, make sure that the **Include nav bar Down state** box is ticked at the top of the **Down** tab of the **Button Editor**.

Making the other buttons

In the **Assets** panel (**Library** tab) you will see your **Button** symbol. Rename it **Planning**.

▶ Drag the button (the name, not the thumbnail) down onto the **New Symbol** icon to create a new button, making sure that the **Kind** is set to **Button**, and call it **Logo**. Repeat this to create buttons called **Birthday Card**, **Dollar**, **Web Page** and **Review**.

New Symbol Icon

▶ Drag an instance of each button onto the canvas. Position them carefully. At this stage they will all say **Planning**, even though you have dragged on five different buttons. You need to change the text in the **Button Editor**.

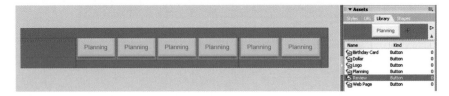

Figure 22.3

 Use the **Properties inspector** to change the **Text** for each of the buttons to reflect its name, as shown in Figure 22.4.

Tip:

For the **Birthday Card** button you will have to double-click it and adjust the position of the text in each button state.

 Save your work so far.

Figure 22.4

Changing the canvas colour

The canvas colour needs to exactly match the eportfolio navigation bar colour. In Dreamweaver, select the navigation bar cell and check the **BG** colour in the **Properties inspector**. Mine is **#3366CC**.

 In Fireworks, click **Modify**, **Canvas**, **Canvas Color**. Click the **Custom Color** box and enter this colour code. Press **Enter**.

Adding the logo

We will put the Base Camp logo in the left-hand corner.

 Open **BaseCampLogoBackground**.

Scale Icon

 Put a circular marquee around it, and copy and paste into your navigation bar in Fireworks. Use the **Scale** tool to size it to fit. Save your file and press **F12** to view it.

Figure 22.5

Exporting the navigation bar

Now we need to export the navigation bar to the eportfolio **HTML_files** folder.

⊙ Click **File**, **Export** and navigate to the **HTML_files** folder.

⊙ Click the **Options** button in the **Export** window. Make sure the **HTML style** is set to **Dreamweaver HTML** and the **Extension** is set to **.html**. Make sure that **Use CSS For Popup Menus** is not ticked. Press **OK**.

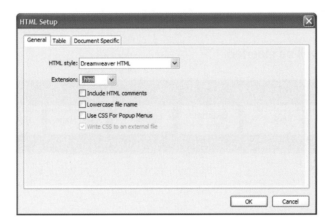

Figure 22.6

⊙ Click the **Put images in subfolder** box and make sure they are going into the **Images** subfolder of **Eportfolio**. (Use the **Browse** button at the bottom of the window.)

⊙ Make sure that **Export** is set to **HTML and Images**, **HTML** is set to **Export HTML File** and **Slices** is set to **Export Slices**.

⊙ Click **Export**.

⊙ In Dreamweaver, open **MainTemplate.dwt** from the **Templates** folder. We will put the navigation bar in the template and it will automatically appear in every page based on this template.

⊙ Click in the top row of the table.

⊙ Click the arrow by the **Insert Picture** button and select **Fireworks HTML**.

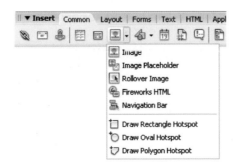

Figure 22.7

Navigate to the **HTML_Files** folder and choose **NavBar.html**. Press **OK**.

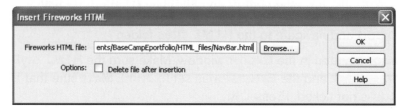

Figure 22.8

The navigation bar will be inserted.

Figure 22.9

Press **Ctrl-S** to save. You will be asked if you want to update files based on this template. Obviously, you do, so click **Update**.

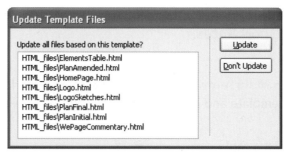

Figure 22.10

In the next window, wait until the **Done** button appears and turns grey, and then click **Close**.

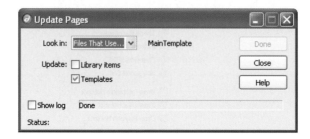

Figure 22.11

You can't preview a template in the browser, because it is a **dwt** file, not an **html** file.

▶ Open the file **HomePage.html**. View the navigation bar in your browser. Test that all the rollover effects work. Close your browser again.

Making the Home button

▶ In Fireworks, save **NavBar.png**. Use **File**, **Save As** to save the file again as **HomeButton.png**.

▶ In Fireworks, delete all six buttons and the logo in **HomeButton.png**.

▶ In the **Library** pane, create a new button, called **Home**, based on one of the existing buttons.

▶ Drag a new instance of this button onto the canvas, and edit the text to read **Home**.

▶ Change the background colour of the canvas to match the bottom left-hand cell of your **MainTemplate**. Mine is the dark blue of the logo: **#000099**.

▶ From the **Menu** bar in Fireworks, select **Modify**, **Canvas**, **Trim Canvas**.

▶ Save the button again.

▶ Export the file, putting the **HomeButton.html** file in the **HTML_files** folder and making sure the images go in the **Images** folder of your eportfolio.

▶ In Dreamweaver, insert the **HomeButton.html** file in the bottom left cell of **MainTemplate**.

▶ Save and update all files using the template.

▶ You can either use the same button on the **SplashPage** template, changing the text to **Enter Site**, or use the brushed steel button, **Button.png**, which you saved in your **Components** folder. Over to you!

Figure 22.12: The Enter Site button on the splash page

 Tip:

When you scale an image with live filters, you will almost certainly need to update the settings.

Adding the links to the Enter and Home buttons

In Dreamweaver, open the **SplashTemplate**. Select the **Enter Site** button. In the **Properties inspector**, drag the **Point to File** icon next to the **Link** box over to **HomePage.html**.

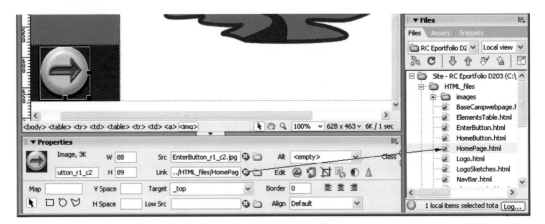

Figure 22.13

Save the template.

Save and update **index.html**. Open **index.html** in a browser and test your button.

Adding the pop-up menus

Open **MainTemplate.dwt**.

Edit with Fireworks Icon

Click the **Planning** button in your navigation bar. In the **Properties inspector**, click the **Edit with Fireworks** button to edit the button in Fireworks.

If you see the following window, click **Use a PNG** and navigate to **NavBar.png**.

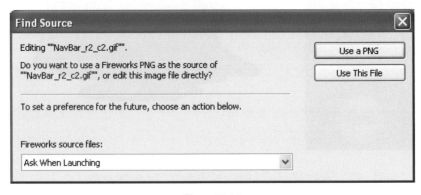

Figure 22.14

Click the **Planning** button in Fireworks to select it.

From the **Menu** bar, select **Modify, Pop-up Menu, Add Pop-up Menu**.

Fill in the name of each pop-up menu item shown in Figure 22.15. We will add the links later. (Click the + symbol to add a new line.)

Figure 22.15

Click **Next**. You can change the appearance of the menu item if you wish – for example, make the text colour the dark blue of the logo. Click **Next**.

Click **Next** to get to the **Position** tab.

Set the pop-up menu position to appear below the button. (You can change this later by dragging it if you need to.)

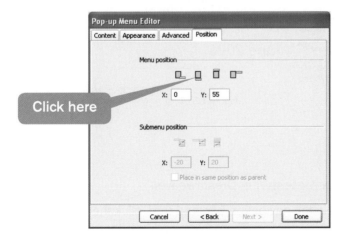

Figure 22.16

Click **Done**. The menu appears as a blue grid, as shown in Figure 22.17.

Figure 22.17

⊚ You will not be able to see the text on the popup menus. Press **F12** to open Internet Explorer, to view your work so far. Try hovering your mouse pointer over the **Planning** button. Close your browser again.

Important Note:

You can edit your pop-up by double-clicking the target on the button.

⊚ Now insert the rest of the pop-up menus from your structure chart (Figure 19.1).

⊚ Click **Done** at the top of the Fireworks window, and return to Dreamweaver.

⊚ Save the template. Update pages made from this template.

⊚ Open **HomePage.html** and save it.

⊚ Press **F12** or **File, Preview in Browser**. Close the browser again once you've tested the menus.

Figure 22.18

Inserting the links

⊚ Switch back to **MainTemplate.dwt** in Dreamweaver.

*Edit with
Fireworks Icon*

⊚ Click any of the buttons in the navigation bar, and then click the **Edit with Fireworks** button in the **Properties inspector**. The navigation bar opens in Fireworks.

⊚ In Fireworks, click the **Planning** button to select it. Double-click the blue frame menu outline that appears.

⊚ Type in the **Link** values using the names of the pages, as shown in Figure 22.19.

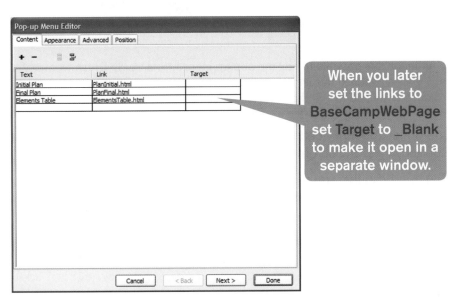

Figure 22:19

Important Note:

The links would be more complicated if the target files were in a different folder. You can use .. to go up a level in the folder hierarchy, if necessary (for example ../other_folder/myfile.html).

- Press **Done** to close the **Pop-up Menu Editor**.
- Click the **Done** button at the top of the Fireworks window to save the changes and return to Dreamweaver.
- Save the template and update the files.

Tip:

If the links don't work, check the **Code** view for **MainTemplate.dwt**. If there are two functions called **mmLoadMenus()** then delete the second one (everything from **function mmLoadMenus()** { up to and including the closing }). Dreamweaver should have done this automatically, but doesn't always get it right. Then save the template, update the dependent html files, and test them again. The links should now work.

- Open **HomePage.html**, save and test in a browser.
- Insert the links in all the other pop-up menus.

Tip:

To make **BaseCampWebPage.html** open in a separate web window, set the **Target** box to **_Blank** (see Figure 22.20).

- You will need to insert the link for the **Review** button, which does not have a pop-up menu.

> **Important Note:**
>
> Although it is possible to edit the pop-up menus from inside Dreamweaver (using the **Behaviors** panel) this is not recommended because you will lose these changes if you later decide to edit the PNG in Fireworks.

Job done! You now need to test the whole eportfolio thoroughly, checking all the content, spelling, links, and so on.

The eportfolio that you can download from the Payne-Gallway website is under 3MB – well within the generous limit of 18MB allowed by Edexcel. This is because every image has been optimized for the eportfolio.

Finally, you need to get feedback on your eportfolio and write your evaluation of it and the project as a whole.

Good Marks... ✓

You will get good marks if:

- your eportfolio is within the limit of 18MB
- all the files are in acceptable formats as listed in the SPB
- all the required evidence, and nothing unnecessary, is included
- links are in consistent styles and positions
- it is easy to navigate around the site
- the commentary on each page explains the evidence clearly
- the text is clear and easy to read
- all the links work even when the links are viewed on another system
- accessibility features are included
- all sources are acknowledged correctly
- you have obtained and acted on feedback from carefully chosen reviewers
- you have thoroughly tested the eportfolio.

Bad Marks... ✗

You will lose marks if:

- you use links to external sites
- the site contains spelling or grammar mistakes
- the images are of poor quality
- the images are very large and take a long time to download.

Chapter 23 – Navigation Nightmares

Creating links in your navigation bar is not always straightforward. The dreaded message **This page cannot be displayed** can pop up infuriatingly when you least expect it. This chapter may help you to solve some of the problems.

Putting the navigation bar in the index.html page

In this eportfolio, we have not put the navigation bar in **index.html**, which is the splash page. In your own project, you may decide not to have a splash page, so the home page will be **index.html**.

You cannot use the same template for the **index.html** page as for the rest of the pages if you use this type of navigation bar with pop-up menus. This is because the **index.html** is in a different folder (the root folder) from all the other pages. Therefore, a path name that works for the content pages will not work for the home page.

For example, the path from **PlanInitial.html** to **PlanFinal.html** will be simply **PlanFinal.html**, as they are both in the same folder. The path from **index.html** to **PlanFinal.html** will be **../ Eportfolio/HTML_files/PlanFinal.html**.

If you don't want a splash page, you can still make a new template, called **HomePageTemplate**, which will look identical to **MainTemplate**, but which has a navigation bar with different links. (All the links will point to files in the **HTML_files** folder rather than to the current folder.)

- Create **HomePageTemplate.dwt**. If you have created it as a copy of **MainTemplate**, delete the existing navigation bar: select the **<td>** containing the bar and press **Delete**. It's also worth using the **Code** view to check that all the JavaScript has been deleted.

- Use Explorer to create a copy of **NavBar.png** (say, **IndexNavBar.png**).

- Export **IndexNavBar** as html, just as you did for **NavBar**. Change the **File name** to **IndexNavBar.html**, otherwise you will overwrite the other one.

- Insert **IndexNavBar.html** into **HomePageTemplate**.

- Create your **index.html** file based on **HomePageTemplate**. Make sure it is saved at the top level of your site.

- Now you can use the **Edit with Fireworks** button to edit your new navigation bar in **HomePageTemplate** without breaking the existing links in pages based on **MainTemplate**.

- You might have to go through the following process several times before you get the links working: update the **HomePageTemplate**'s menu using **Edit with Fireworks**, save the template and update **index.html**, open **index.html** in a browser and test the links.

- Carefully check that all the other links in your eportfolio are working too.

Index

Index

Index